Madonna King is one of Australia's most accomplished journalists, having won awards for her *ABC Mornings* current affairs programme. She writes across Fairfax, *Crikey* and *The New Daily*, and is the author of ten books, including the bestselling *Being 14* (ABIA shortlisted for non-fiction book of the year) and *Fathers and Daughters*. She is also the biographer of 2006 Australian of the Year Professor Ian Frazer and former federal treasurer Joe Hockey. In 2018, Madonna served as chair of the Queensland Government's Anti-Cyberbullying Taskforce, set up in the wake of COAG. A fellow of the prestigious World Press Institute, she has served as a visiting fellow at the Queensland University of Technology and on the Walkley Advisory Board. Her website, www.madonnaking.com.au, provides further detail. She lives in Brisbane with her husband and two teenage daughters.

 @madonnamking

ALSO BY MADONNA KING

*Think Smart Run Hard: Lessons in Business
Leadership from Maxine Horne*

Hockey: Not Your Average Joe

Ian Frazer: The Man Who Saved a Million Lives

*A Generous Helping: Treasured Recipes from the
People of Queensland* (with Alison Alexander)

Bali 9: The Untold Story (with Cindy Wockner)

*Catalyst: The Power of the Media and
the Public to Make Change*

*Being 14: Helping Fierce Teens
Become Awesome Women*

*Fathers and Daughters: Helping Girls and
Their Dads Build Unbreakable Bonds*

MADONNA KING

TEN-AGER

What your daughter needs you to know
about the transition from child to teen

First published in Australia and New Zealand in 2021
by Hachette Australia Pty Ltd

First published in Great Britain in 2021
by Headline Home
an imprint of Headline Publishing Group

1

Cataloguing in Publication Data is available from the British Library

ISBN 978 14722 8526 3
eISBN 978 14722 8527 0

Cover design by Christabella Designs
Author photograph: Tyler Alberti
Text design by Bookhouse

Typeset in 12.2/18.6 pt Sabon LT Std by Bookhouse, Sydney
Printed and bound in Great Britain by Clays Ltd, Elcograf S.p.A.

Headline's policy is to use papers that are natural, renewable and
recyclable products and made from wood grown in sustainable forests.
The logging and manufacturing processes are expected to conform
to the environmental regulations of the country of origin.

HEADLINE PUBLISHING GROUP
An Hachette UK Company
Carmelite House
50 Victoria Embankment
London EC4Y 0DZ

www.headline.co.uk
www.hachette.co.uk

To all our ten-year-old girls. The victory is so much sweeter when you run your own race.

Contents

Preface

Olivia is writing a list of goals for this week. *1) MAKE FRIENDS!* This was number two on last week's list, but has proved more difficult than she thought since she swapped from her primary school to middle school last year. *2) ASK MUM FOR A PHONE.* It's second this week after falling a notch, but she's not giving up. She will pester her parents today and tomorrow and the next day because she is the *only* one, she says, in her class without one. Once she gets a phone, she's going to get TikTok and then her life will be perfect. Almost. Some of her other goals are more secret. She hasn't written down that she wants to lose weight, because her mother would get angry like she did the first time she saw her new cursive writing commit it to paper. But she does want to. And she wants to be shorter, too. That's probably why some of the girls don't want to be her friend: she is too tall. Maybe that accounts for the teasing. Emmy laughed at her last week, on the day they were allowed to wear their pyjamas to school. 'Who's wearing Disney pyjamas?' She'd spat out that question almost like an accusation, and everyone looked at her. *Everyone.* Now Olivia keeps her pyjamas under her pillow. *3) ASK MUM FOR NEW PYJAMAS.*

Olivia could be your daughter or mine; our niece or best friend's daughter or granddaughter. She is ten and lives in cities and towns the nation over. Her thoughts and feelings, like those of her peers, teeter between childhood and womanhood. She's a ten-ager: the new teenager, in a world of instant learning and connectivity, where the power of celebrity reigns, where the online world envelops decision-making and where friends can turn into foes over lunchtime. She's seeing a bigger world and all the opportunities and challenges it offers, but she needs to be cared for and nurtured and hugged. She needs to be encouraged to reach for her own stars, not those of the A-student sitting next to her. And she needs us – her parents and others in her life – to listen, without judgement. She'll explain why in the pages that follow.

In Australia, ten-year-olds don't face the same challenges as some of their peers in other parts of the world: banned from education, sold into slavery, marked for marriage a year or two later. That is just execrable, but it doesn't mean that our own daughters, going to school in Sydney and Melbourne and Geelong and Perth and Adelaide, are finding today effortless and uncomplicated. Some days, as they explain, are burdensome and daunting and downright hard as they navigate their own journey into adulthood. And they need our help, even if they don't ask for it.

A ten-year-old girl is precious. Wide-eyed and willing to learn. Wanting to help. Wanting to please. Wanting to fix the environment. Wanting to be heard. She's likely to be more worldly than her parents were at this age, but less independent. She's well-read, and the music she listens to and the television programs she follows are full of good things, mostly. But *how* she listens and watches – and the pervasive influence of the online world and the messages it carries – is more challenging. And it's a world, and an influence, that is difficult for any parent to really understand. Feminism, for our daughters, is different: it doesn't have to be argued; they know they are equal to their male peers. Social justice is different, too. Theirs is a world where most are disarmingly non-judgemental of others ... and agonisingly judgemental of themselves. There, the judgement can be unimaginably harsh.

If Olivia's mum were writing her goals for the week, they'd revolve around her ten-year-old. 'I'd want her to smile more.' 'I'd want her to like herself more.' 'I'd want her to believe enough is enough.' This project was born out of *Being 14*, a book chronicling the specific challenges facing the fourteen-year-old cohort of girls. But parents, particularly mothers, asked me to look earlier. They wanted me to find out what was happening at ten, when their daughter was showing a touch of attitude along with a new social conscience, a worldliness, without the analytical skills to decipher real from fake. An age where some of their daughters were just beginning to wriggle out of hugs and into the privacy of their own rooms. An age where they would do anything to fit in.

To those girls and their peers – in big places and small, in cities and on rural properties – who allowed me into their lives, thank you. Almost 500 of them, across Australia, answered my questions, wrote me notes and sat around tables having discussions to help me under-stand what they really wanted their parents to know. My take-out is that despite the vulnerabilities and challenges being faced by our ten-agers, our future is in the most marvellous, caring and clever hands.

This is a book for their parents. It includes the views of 1600 mothers and draws on the experience of 400 dads. Educators, too, have been invaluable, and in addition to school principals, counsellors and psychologists, almost one hundred Year 5, 6 and 7 public and private school teachers have explained how they see the ten-year-old girls sitting in front of them. Their insights made me smile and frown in equal measure: girls wanting to learn everything, but be liked at all costs; girls wanting to act years older than they should, but who burst out crying too easily; girls wielding their popularity like a weapon, but who were lost finding allies.

Over the next eighteen chapters you'll meet experts on sleep and puberty, friendship and self-harm, on education and resilience and a dozen other issues. They have all given their time to answer question after question about Olivia and her ten-year-old peers in the hope that we will listen to them more, and understand them better. That's what they want, and I know that because they told me.

Who are our ten-agers?

'I often wish that I could take their dreams and say, "Look I'm just going to preserve this for you. And when you're fourteen and fifteen, you can come back here and open up that bottle and see what that young girl wanted and dreamt of."'

Andrew Fuller, psychologist and author

Meet Layla. She's ten and sassy and smart. She also describes herself as funny and kind, and she loves to dance. So does her friend Sofia, although Sofia's giving it up next month. She doesn't look good, she says, in her dance outfit, and she's too busy anyway. She also received a smartphone for her tenth birthday, and is the envy of her 'group' – a merry-go-round of peers who can be friends and foes during the same school day. She says she struggles to belong sometimes, and wishes she was as good at school as Tahlia, who sits next to her. Tahlia moved schools last year, to a new 'middle school' for Years 5 and 6, and she too struggles to find friends. 'I'm a bit annoying and I'm also too tall,' she says. Claire understands. But she's more focused on convincing her parents that she needs a smartphone, like Sofia. 'I am the only one in my whole group who doesn't have one,' she says.

Layla and Sofia and Tahlia and Claire. Four girls out of 500 who shared with me their secret hopes and dreams, the challenges they face when they wake up, and what keeps them from sleeping some nights. Together, they paint a delightful picture of our ten-year-old daughters, sisters, nieces and grandchildren. With brutal honesty, they describe finding friends on the journey to finding themselves – their biggest challenge. At ten, their brains and bodies are altering in ways that are not all visible. Self-confidence can arm them some days, and disarm them on others. Believing in themselves seemed easier a couple of years ago, when they took centre stage with gusto, even charging family and friends to see them dance and sing. Now they worry about how others judge them. So many things are changing at this age, they told me, including their parents! In a bid to find their own identity, they look beyond Mum and Dad to other role models. The imperative to fit in is compelling; they see that as the golden ticket to friendship.

This is Generation Alpha, as social researcher Mark McCrindle calls them – the front-end of a new cohort born since 2010 and moulded by unique times. They were born a few years after the smartphone came out, and in the same year that the first-generation iPad was released and Instagram launched. Siri and AirPods, streaming and TikTok, Instagram and YouTube will be part of their teenage DNA. 'Not only are these ten-year-olds a cohort, an age group, but in so many ways a metaphor for the future,' McCrindle says. 'They're almost a lens. They are living the future before we have even seen it.' Having had screens as pacifiers since birth, their world is different – even from their Gen Z big sisters. For this post-key, post-cash generation, the world has moved from written to visual media – aka Instagram, TikTok and YouTube – and the muscular influence it has. Globally connected, our ten-agers will have opportunities galore. But digital literacy risks stunting their social growth and means they might not be as well equipped to live life as their parents were. 'Going for a bushwalk or camping or even getting a campfire organised is something that is beyond the skills of many,' McCrindle says. Courses and school excursions have often replaced childhood adventures. That's partly a reflection of the way we parent, but also of a change in the make-up of our cities and the lure of medium- and high-density living, which has killed off big backyards. Life is more structured, too, and after-school tutoring, soccer coaching and gymnastics sessions have taken over from the free play of earlier generations. The focus of parents, often, is towards academic outcomes, and with busy lives themselves, family time tends to see every minute filled.

Today's ten-year-olds are on the brink of adolescence and all the wonders it brings. But as girls from Perth, Sydney, Hobart, Brisbane, Melbourne and so many other places in between told me, adolescence also presents mountain-sized obstacles. There's navigating self-confidence and resilience when tears seem easier. There's the body image issues that saturate decision-making. There's new school workloads. There's anxiety. And then there's friendships. Making friends used to be like eating a piece of cake: easy, delicious and comforting. Now it's different. Some have cake and others don't. Some share and some don't. Some don't like their sort of cake.

Many girls, at ten, describe the challenges they face with precocious eloquence. Others are still finding the words. But here's the thing about this cohort: differences in development and maturity – in the same class and even in the same friendship circle – can make for long days and short nights. Some girls, at ten, still believe in unicorns, the warm hand of their dad on the walk through the school gates, and the Build-A-Bear they received last Christmas. Others are shaving their legs, offering their opinions on Snapchat and wondering whether the boy on the bus likes them. Kellie Lyneham, deputy principal (student wellbeing) at Melbourne's Korowa Anglican Girls' School, sees this wide variance in development regularly. 'There's a critical mass who want to be treated like grown-up girls, who want to have the opportunities to demonstrate independence and to make choices about their learning and about their experience on a daily basis,' she says. 'But then there's a cohort who would really just like to be treated like little girls.'

Author and teen educator Dannielle Miller sees that diversity as striking at this age. 'Some look physically very small and are very interested in ponies and glitter. And others look quite grown-up; they're probably already on that puberty journey.' She's reminded of Britney Spears's 'I'm Not a Girl, Not Yet a Woman', and says the age of ten has become the new thirteen. We now have ten-agers. A few years ago, when speaking at schools to teenagers, she focused on body image and friendship and deconstructing the culture around womanhood. 'Now schools are calling me and saying, '"This is happening in Year 4." Everything is happening earlier,' she says.

Kevin Tutt, formerly the principal of Seymour College in Adelaide, has been an educator and school leader across boys', girls' and co-ed schools for decades. He says, 'Childhood is short and the societal pressure on young girls to be more teenage-like, even more womanly, is quite frightening.' He is troubled, too, by some parents encouraging the rush to adulthood. 'The parties that some ten-year-old girls are now going to – they're very teenagey, even adult-like, and that's quite worrying.'

So is the coronavirus, which will shape our ten-year-olds going forward, in the same way World War II, the Great Depression and September 11 have shaped other generations. 'Hitting ten years of age when schools are shutting, when globally the economy moves into recession, which we haven't seen for three decades, and when all of the normalities of life have come to a screeching halt – that will be the profoundest of influences,' Mark McCrindle says. That cannot be underestimated this year or next year or the year after that. Teachers are seeing it in the stories being submitted and in class artwork. Parents are reporting disrupted sleep patterns and increased anxiety. Girls have seen a health crisis become an economic crisis, which has an impact on who they socialise with and how they do that. 'I'm worried it will get to Mum and Dad,' one girl told me. In the two years to December 2019, Kids Helpline told me ten-year-olds made contact 4091 times. Girls made 70 per cent of those calls. But during the first four months of 2020, when we grappled with the pandemic, those figures increased 24 per cent – with ten-year-olds asking about family relationships, emotional wellbeing and mental health. With schools closed, interestingly, the number of calls about friendships and bullying dropped.

Being ten now is like being thirteen a few years ago; children are older, younger. And those first steps away from their parents' embrace are met by a new wall of influence: the power of peers, and unnamed influencers who now make up a $10 billion online celebrity marketing world. Social media, whether a girl has a smartphone or peeks at her friend's, will shape much of her decision-making – from what jeans she wants to wear to what music she wants to play. The birthday gift de jour for ten-year-olds during lockdown was a smartphone. Of course, not all parents were in a position to afford one, but in this research it was a common present. Parents wanted to ensure their daughters stayed in contact with friends. In some cases, it worked a treat. In many other instances, it became a purgatory for the whole family and a new avenue both for bullying and isolation. But certainly, when schools resumed after the first lockdown, teachers noticed how some girls were struggling with socialisation skills. 'We do a lot of work on the socialisation of the girls, and we do a lot of work in Grade 5 on being a friend, making new friends, what to do when friends have conflict, and we work through all of those processes so carefully,' says Catherine O'Kane, principal of Brisbane's All Hallows' School. The smartphone – and in particular the iPhone, which came out in 2007 – has moulded this cohort. O'Kane offers this reminder to the parents of ten-agers: 'I think my daughter, who's twenty-seven, got a cassette player for her twelfth birthday. At the time I remember thinking, "Well, I'm such an indulgent mother." It was a cassette player, for heaven's sake!' Now, smart-phone technology is ubiquitous. 'It's just like water,' she says. So too are the challenges it can present, according to educators. Sexualised behaviour. Changes in language. A race to grow up. Seeing things that young minds don't quite understand. Instant gratification, which means some of the mysteries of adolescence are gone. Bullying. No down-time. Increased anxiety. The fear of missing out. Lost sleep. Minds that won't turn off. Comparisons with photo-doctored celebrities. The list goes on.

So who do they go to with their problems? Sometimes Mum and Dad. Sometimes Nan and Pop, who offer less judgement. But increasingly, it is friends. Sometimes, now, they'll keep their own secrets rather than blurting them out. 'I don't even tell anyone, even if they're my family,' says one girl. 'I'm just scared if they judge me for who I am. So I keep quiet when there's a problem . . . I know it's bad but I feel that I can't trust anyone, not even myself sometimes.' But it's also difficult for many parents, with the pressure to keep up with Sienna, Grace, Jasmine, Chloe and the growing number of friends at school who are brandishing a new phone. 'Can you please write a chapter on why all my friends have a phone and I don't?' one ten-year-old pleaded. She, along with her peers, can wield pressure like a pro. Unrelenting. She'll pout and sulk and tell her parents they don't understand; the world has changed. And it has.

Their parents are Gen Y-ers (or millennials) mainly, with the median age of a mother giving birth now exceeding thirty-one years. In this research, parents' ages ranged from thirty-one to fifty-nine. The birth rate is dropping, too, and many ten-year-olds now have fewer siblings than previous generations.

The ten-ager's parents see her as kind and sassy and chatty and dreamy and sensitive. Also funny and sporty and musical and a delight. 'She's a mixed bag of everything,' one parent says. She's also mean to her sister, and wanting more time to herself, she wears her heart on her sleeve, and she wants to find her place with friends. She can be bossy and shy, extroverted at home and introverted at school. 'A grumpy little rebel with an equally gorgeous heart,' says one parent. 'In a rush to grow up,' says another. A leader. A follower. A worrier. An over-thinker. Too anxious. Too teary. 'At this age she is a delight,' one mother says. 'She can be grown up and trying on make-up – then turn around and bounce on a trampoline for hours, giggling with her bestie. We have seen flashes of hormones kick in. Her body is changing, legs are long, breasts are starting to develop. I am just adoring this lovely age and cherishing every moment, as I know it will change soon.' But she has a lament: 'I'm sad that this generation of kids never got to have the freedom – experiences both good and bad – of being let loose and growing up with other kids roaming the streets and parks, like we did in the 1980s. This generation is so scheduled, organised, online.' Online. TikTok. Insta. YouTube. 'Why are some still into Barbies and playing babies and others want to be teenagers already?' another mother asks.

Their parents know it's a different world for their daughters. 'It's such a stark comparison parenting our children after the way we were brought up. It's so confusing,' one says. 'It seems like good old values are harder to instil in my children, like gratefulness, ethical standards and being polite.' And another: 'I do wonder what's become of this generation that's dissolved the respect that kids used to have for adult figures. Teachers have maintained it but I don't know a child who behaves with the respect we used to have towards [other] adults.' Or: 'She's a lot more grown up than I was. Puberty has started a lot earlier and she's dealing with the changes and hormones much earlier than I did.' 'I was much more motivated to be outside and try my best at everything,' another says, and adds, 'My ten-year-old just wants to look at herself in the mirror and wear clothes that her friends do.' But she is more articulate, older, anxious. 'I think my daughter is much more mature than I was at that age,' one mother says.

Like flower buds opening up to the sun, ten-year-olds need to be nurtured and guided as their roots take hold.

Not as much as when they were seedlings, but enough to learn how to live amongst the weeds and endure the bouts of bad weather that will challenge them through adolescence and beyond. This is the age when they start to be influenced by individuals outside their family. Toni Riordan, the principal of Brisbane's St Aidan's Anglican Girls' School, sees the way in which friends start to play a much bigger role, describing girls of this age as 'little bowerbirds' in search of their own identity. An infinite online world provides constant challenges to their decision-making, along with their independence, resilience and self-esteem. Riordan says older students also influence the young ones. 'It's always about the big girls. "What are the big girls doing? How are they sitting? Are they wearing their uniform? What sport are they playing?"' Paulina Skerman, the principal of Sydney's Santa Sabina College, says 'The Greta effect' has resulted in more ten- and eleven-year-olds now being involved in social justice and environmental issues than she can ever remember. But it comes with a flip side, she says. 'With that involvement comes a fear about the world. We want them thinking about the world and making their mark and looking at how they're going to be as adults, be part of the solution, but it's a massive responsibility to put on a little person who is ten. So we have to do it in a way that they're really not afraid of growing up.'

'I think my daughter is much more anxious than I was at ten,' one mother says, and that's mirrored widely. She's busier, less resilient and faces more expectations. 'She is much more aware of people's opinions, body image and clothes, but she is also more socially aware of inequality and global issues.' The girls proffer Malala Yousafzai and Michelle Obama as idols, alongside Billie Eilish and Taylor Swift. Worryingly, they believe most of what someone online – including an advertiser – tells them. They are convinced that the shampoo they saw on Instagram will treat both oily roots and dry ends, or that the holiday destination seen on Snapchat looks like that in real life. 'I was carefree,' one mother says of herself at ten. And you know her daughter doesn't feel the same way. 'My daughter is less able to amuse herself than I was at ten,' another says. She's also so much busier than her mother. 'The workload and number of extracurricular activities is crazy, and she seems to have so much more pressure than I did at ten. All I did after school was watch cartoons and drink Milo.' And: 'At ten, I was playing in piles of dirt with my dog, riding my bike, playing with a pet chicken and goat in the bush.'

Some are doing that. Many are not. But at ten, a girl knows she is changing. So many told me they want the independence to make their own decisions, like to go to bed later than their parents say, but admit they grapple with the consequences of being tired the next day. They want privacy in their own room – except when the corona-virus presents an ugly uncertainty and they want Mum or Dad to lie with them until they fall asleep. Often, they don't know where they fit in with others. 'I just want to find a good friend' – that line was delivered by so many girls.

The University of Melbourne's Professor Susan Sawyer, who is president of the International Association of Adolescent Health, says 'everything is happening for ten-year-olds girls'. Similar to a swan gliding on water, she says, we can't see what's happening in the murky water below. Their body began the first stages of puberty years earlier; now their brain is changing too. They can feel fantastic one minute and at a loss the next. Their friends can paradoxically also be their tormentors. They can look in the mirror and see a distorted image they don't like: they are too tall, or too fat, or their nose is wrong. They can decide they are a 'maths girl' or not, the 'sporty type' or not – way too early. They can let others determine their potential before they begin their own teenage-hood. New Zealand school counsellor Marcelle Nader-Turner describes a ten-year-old as 'teetering on the brink of leaving her childhood behind and facing the world as a young woman'.

Phyllis Fagell, student counsellor and author of *Middle School Matters*, calls it 'straddling' childhood and adolescence. One moment she will be light-hearted and happy-go-lucky; the next, a deep, dark, introspective adolescent. 'They are already going through or close to puberty. They are very much interested in having a voice and feeling confident and exercising autonomy and feeling independent and being respected.' They want to make a contribution to the world, too. 'They want to right wrongs,' says Fagell. 'They want to address injustice, and they're often this very unique blend of malleable, impressionable, naive and sophisticated – intellectual and capable of deep insight.' That brings back the difficulty of co-existing in a class where the maturity gap is wide, and this makes ten-year-olds perhaps the least homogeneous – in some ways but not others – of any school class. Because some are playing with dolls and some are 'ranking their crushes', there can be a sense of melancholy amongst those who think their peers are leaving them behind, says Fagell. That's just one variable put to the test as they search for their friendship tribe. St Margaret's Anglican Girls School principal Ros Curtis says that often the younger girls feel as though 'they're missing out on something'. 'By the age of ten, some can provide context and you start to get real polar opposites in that age group,' she says. Melbourne Girls Grammar principal Dr Toni Meath says sometimes the girls will move between those stages as they grow. 'They'll still dip back into that imaginary play ... but then they can code-switch, depending on what they're faced with as well.' She says you can see it at sleepovers, when imagination will rule some games, before they break out the music videos and start dancing. Karen Spiller, a long-time principal who heads Brisbane's John Paul College, says often we treat them in a 'childish manner'. 'I think we can fall very easily into the trap of not having high enough expectations of what they can do, what they can achieve and what they can be,' she says. But community judgement on these girl-women can be tough. Melbourne educator Kellie Lyneham sees that in her own child. 'I think there's something to grieve – that our tall, beautiful little girl is going to be perceived by the community as much older and more sophisticated than we really want her to be.'

Developmental neuroscientist Dr Hannah Kirk flags being ten as difficult. 'It's not as though they've got established brain structures that allow them to easily engage in social interactions,' she says. 'Everyone's a learning process at this stage.' Furthermore, 'They're having to do a lot of trial and error. Does this work in this situation? Does this not work? They're building up that library for themselves to go back to and refer to later on. This is that critical stage where they are going through a lot of new experiences and therefore having to make a lot of mistakes as well – and that can be very challenging.' That makes resilience skills important: they need to learn by failing – which can also help brain development. 'It's refining those neural connections through trial and error. When we get a strategy we know works then we continue to use that strategy, and it's through that process that we see stronger connections being built.' Kirk also raises the influence of friends. 'They still feel close to their parents but are starting to shift towards their friends, and this will continue and peak in high school, around the age of fourteen,' she says.

School – whether primary school or a middle school between junior and high – is crucial to how this year will play out. 'I feel like at this age they're just a sponge,' says Tara McLachlan, school psychologist at Brisbane Girls Grammar School. 'But they're also just untainted. It's about fostering that and encouraging them to do whatever they want to do, and teaching them the resilience skills to be able to deal with whatever high school throws at them, or life in general.' Year 5 teachers paint an illuminating picture of the girls in their classes. 'They need to fit in, to be the same and to be liked at all costs,' one says. 'Some girls won't be who they are because the popular girls make them feel bad,' says another. And a third teacher says, 'How social issues amongst friends affect how these girls perform in the classroom – this seems to be one of the biggest distractions in our entire cohort.' What are some other issues teachers rank as making our ten-agers delightful and demanding in equal measure? Tears. Anxiety. A lack of resilience. Curious minds. Learning to work in teams. Friendship fall-outs. The difficulty of three girls playing well together. Silent bullying. Isolating peers. Gossip. A lack of self-worth. Big smiles at the opportunities on offer.

Phyllis Fagell says ten-year-old girls 'are as confusing to themselves as they are to the adults who are reading them'. *They*, and their parents, want answers, and their questions are all quite similar.

These are from girls, all aged ten:

'When can we have social media, because I feel left out?'

'How can I tell Mum I need a phone?'

'Why do I find it hard to make friends who stay with me?'

'Can you do a chapter on when is the age when you start to want a boyfriend?'

'How do I make my mum and dad listen to me?'

Their parents asked these questions, and many others that were similar:

'How can I help her to become an independent problem-solver who can shrug it off when someone criticises her?'

'How can I prepare her and teach her to protect herself from how cruel other kids can be both at school and online?'

'How can we empower them to make good choices and stand up for what they think is right?'

'I'd love to know what they want their parents to know.'

'Are they happy? I think my daughter is happy but she tells stories that make me think some of her peers aren't. I'd like to know if it's common for this age group to be miserable about themselves.'

'Why is childhood so short?'

2

Body and brain

'Sometimes I feel like this is the calm before
the storm. My daughter is so funny and so
completely herself right now. I hope that puberty
doesn't change that confidence and clarity
she has. I also hope she sees me as a support
and not an enemy during the years ahead.'

Mother of a tween

Puberty starts up to six years before a girl's first period. That time, when we can't see what's happening, is an important marker to how she will fare as a teen. Understanding it better might lead to changing her trajectory in areas like mental health and disease. These are just a few points George Patton, Professor of Adolescent Health Research at the University of Melbourne, wants us to know. A world leader in the area, he and his team have spent almost a decade probing the beginnings of puberty and how it unfolds: why children reach it at varying ages and stages, the impact it has, and how understanding it could change many of their trajectories. The Childhood to Adolescence Transition Study (CATS), which began in 2012 and includes more than 1200 children, families and teachers in and around Melbourne, already offers up a stark reminder that we have to reorient our views on puberty away from the focus on a girl's first period to when it might really begin.

The next few pages are less about what our ten-year-olds are saying and more about what is happening in their minds and bodies; much of which they – or we – don't understand. It's about what's happening 'underneath the bonnet', as Professor Patton describes it, and is crucial to how we see them and deal with them, and their path forward. And it's Professor Patton's knowledge that might make all the difference to many of our daughters. The early stages of puberty, he says, are as invisible as they are important, and that's why his team is following children annually, measuring all aspects of pubertal development, including first hormonal maturation – the adrenal maturation, which varies between children but begins often around the ages of seven and eight. Before the arrival of menarche, or a girl's first period, our daughters travel a journey that's more complex than the appearance of body hair, breast buds and a growth spurt would suggest. In

Professor Patton's words, 'it's a profoundly life-changing event'. 'Periods are important because it's a late event, but there's a hell of a lot that's happening beforehand. What we've come to understand is that puberty is a process which unfolds over half a dozen years.'

That first phase of adrenal maturation is more pivotal than previously thought, in terms of metabolic development and later-life risks for things like obesity and polycystic ovarian syndrome. 'We think this is probably a really important age where you may be able to change trajectories,' Patton says. Lights are going on in the brain here, and a child begins to develop a sense of who they're going to be in the world. It's a time where they will reorient themselves away from family and towards their peer group. It's a time when concerns about body image might first emerge. 'That has real significance, not only of risks later, like eating disorders, but also in terms of girls being sensitive about their bodies. We see this process across puberty and continuing into later adolescence, and girls beginning to reduce their physical activity,' he says. Everything he says here is borne out in the answers of the girls interviewed for this book. Reorienting away from their families: 'I talk to my best friends now more because I can trust them and they would help me through [anything],' one says. 'I would talk to my Mum about my problems, but also my friends now,' says another. Concerns about body image: 'I worry about how I look,' one says.

'I'm too tall,' another says in explaining why she can't find friends. 'I worry I'm fat,' says another.

Different cultures deal with puberty differently. In some, girls become more protected or are encouraged to hide themselves from public view. In others, the whole process is a celebration of a girl becoming a woman, a rite of passage. And in others again – and perhaps big chunks of the western world fit here – it's coloured by an attitude of benign neglect, as evidenced by the fact that many girls fear its arrival. Often the first period is not a cause of celebration in a home, and frequently a tween will ask that her dad not be told of its arrival. 'Just don't tell Dad!' a friend's daughter pleaded with her mother. 'Do you promise?' While there are many mothers who still avoid talking to their daughters about periods until they are nine or ten, there are also many girls who refuse to talk to either parent about puberty. They don't want to hear about it or know about it. It's as though they are turning their back on the idea of growing up, holding on tight to childhood. An understanding that puberty doesn't start and stop with a period could help girls – and also their parents and teachers. Professor Patton says that his study, which tracks children through puberty from eight to sixteen, looks at the biological, social and emotional influences during puberty, and might help teachers understand 'something they can't really put their finger on' but that takes hold in Years 3 and 4. 'Teachers are important figures in the lives of kids. I don't think this is something that teachers are generally trained in,' he says. 'But in terms of teaching and kids reorienting themselves to the wider world, this is an incredible opportunity for education systems to be providing and guiding that sort of reorientation.'

This first stage is also crucial in terms of a girl's mental health, including her ability to interact with peers and develop solid social skills. Sometimes, here, girls will not only reorient themselves away from family towards peers, but perhaps work less, and shun being a 'good girl'. And all this leads into another phase of puberty, the start of gonadal maturation, which is what we might typically think of as puberty. This is the phase that leads, later, to the development of periods, and can vary in duration from four to five years. In practical terms, you might see this phase in the emotions a girl shows, as a cascade of changes occurs in her brain. You might see attitude and anger and anxiety and the need for privacy. You might see your daughter feel uncomfortable and irritable, and show an interest in the opposite sex. 'If you are writing a book,' one ten-year-old asked me, 'can you include when it's time to like a boy and how do you know if they like you back?' Invisible changes can have a bigger impact on a girl in the lead-up to her first period than the arrival of that first period. The CATS study is seeking answers to the questions posed by many of our tweens, including understanding a rise in both obesity and mental health problems. 'Why is it that there are so many kids today who are suffering with problems, particularly girls? Problems with depression and anxiety are through the roof in some schools. Self-harm is common. We are looking at all of this,' Professor Patton says.

This work is consequential in appreciating our ten- and eleven-year-old girls and how they see themselves, their peers and the world around them. It's an examination of a developmental group that hasn't been researched as thoroughly as some others, like infants or toddlers, for example. 'We've put all our eggs into that basket,' Professor Patton says. 'But if you wanted to create the Ash Barty of the next generation, you could invest in all you could afford in the first three years of life and you'd never get an Ash Barty. But if you invest about the ages of seven and eight, when the motor cortex is actually developing, if you invest then in tennis lessons and training, you might just get an Ash Barty, because that is the sensitive time of them developing.' None of this means skills can't be learnt at earlier or later stages, but this is the period when children are 'programmed' to pick up skills, particularly social and emotional ones. That's a lesson for public policy makers as much as for educators and parents. 'It's no surprise that this is the age where, if things go wrong, mental health problems emerge,' Professor Patton says.

'By and large, the kids who get to those [mental health] services at the ages of fifteen to sixteen have already had mental health issues from the ages of seven and eight. For half their life they've had these problems – so we're not really doing early intervention. We are intervening really quite late in the process. We're missing the boat.'

The impacts of those under-the-bonnet changes are popping up in bedrooms and lounge rooms, at family gatherings and in classrooms across the nation. 'Out of nowhere, it feels like the hormones have kicked in,' one mother of a ten-year-old says. 'She seemed to go from child to tween overnight. She has become more passionate about her female friends and seems much more head-strong – almost like she feels more insightful about the world than her mum!' Sound familiar? At ten, not many of those quizzed had had their first period, although for some girls it had arrived as early as seven. Professor Susan Sawyer says that 'everything is happening for ten-year-old girls' in the lead-up to their first period . . . there is a lot of activity happening underneath in the brain, but we're not yet necessarily seeing a whole lot of visibility of the secondary sexual characteristics or the linear growth spurt.'

This is what some mothers see of the changes happening in their daughters:

'I think she's starting to think about boys more, as other girls at school were talking about boys.'

'She is valuing her friends' opinions more.'

'She says she is ugly.'

'She's so hormonal!'

'Friends are more important to her than they have been. Her emotions have wilder swings. I'm losing the glimpses of the innocent, playful kid of only a year ago.'

'She will get tired and frustrated at the end of the day and can raise her voice or tear up easily over small things.'

'She's hormonal, more certain of what she likes and doesn't like, and enjoys playing with make-up. She's more sensitive about things.'

'She cries at the drop of a hat over silly things. And answers back more.'

'Definitely hormonal changes. Greasy hair, short-tempered, friendships are more important than when she was younger, she's less likely to just make friends with new kids at the park. Crying more.'

'We sped from Harry Potter to cool girls' fashion in a short time space.'

Many parents would concur with these observations. They might also note the first of the 'I'm fat' comments and observe the way awareness of the judgement of peers over outfits and haircuts, and even the sound of her voice, affects their daughter's choices. There's mood swings, attitude, eye-rolling and demands for more privacy. Their ten-year-old begins pulling away, saying 'no' and finding her parents – especially Dad – a tad embarrassing.

None of these things surprise Amanda Dunn, Melbourne journalist and author of *The New Puberty*. She says puberty can be tough for many because it changes both girls' bodies and how they see themselves as young people. 'It is a time when mental health issues can come to the fore, when self-esteem can plummet and when risk-taking can override good sense,' she says. When she speaks to parents about puberty, the sexualisation of young girls is usually raised. With a daughter herself, Dunn understands that. The marketing of what is 'male' and what is 'female' starts before birth, she says, and continues through childhood and adolescence. 'Girls get the message to be passive, pink and pretty, boys to be active and loud and strong,' she writes. 'You only have to walk into a toy store these days to be overwhelmed by its pinkness for girls, the way every item seems to be accompanied by butterflies or fairies or ponies, while the boys are given pirates and trucks and dinosaurs.'[1] She says it is a school's job to teach children about their bodies and their sexual maturation 'as much as it is their job to teach kids about long division'. Years 3 and 4 are the best time to start, and it is important to label body parts with their correct names. (Other experts also recommend body parts be called by their correct names, some saying it leads to higher self-esteem and a healthier body image, and even reduces the chance of being tricked into online sexual activity.)

Professor Susan Sawyer says it is the more progressive schools that are prepared to engage in conversations around sex education in primary school. 'That obviously needs to happen if the median age of menarche is twelve and a half years. That means that 50 per cent of girls are going to be menstruating before the age of twelve and a half. We need to have these conversations in primary school for both boys and girls.' Sawyer's mother, almost ninety and a retired GP, says that for her as a teenager, menstruation was not even talked about with friends. Dunn says, 'It's no good waiting until a girl discovers she's bleeding one day and thinks she's dying – countless renditions of which you will hear from women who went through puberty just a few generations ago.'

That's exactly what happened at St Columba's in Dalby, when one of my friends first bled in Year 5. A group of us, thinking she was gravely ill, slinked out of the school grounds to the ambulance station across the road, looking for reassurance. We were sent on our way quickly, with advice from the ambulance officer (who could have been the age of any of our fathers) that she wasn't dying and that we should consult our mothers. Mothers. Not fathers. Menstrual educator and author Jane Bennett, who created the workshop Celebration Day for Girls, says puberty needs to be celebrated and that males need to play a role in this. 'We live in a society where we still have a considerable menstrual taboo and a menstrual shame,' she says. Rather than passing on their own embarrassment and shame, parents should be encouraged to provide the emotional support and information that will boost their daughter's confidence. 'If a mother or father or both could genuinely say "congratulations", it's so much more than most women ever had,' Bennett says. 'Genuinely be positive and loving and warm, and then just do what comes naturally . . . you can pay for dinner that night, or a hot chocolate. You might, over the next couple of months, have a special little party with the women in the family. It can be any number of things. It doesn't have to be elaborate; it's the spirit of the thing.' It also makes a 'massive difference' to girls if fathers show they understand and are willing to help out by buying sanitary products, or keeping spare pads in the glove box of the car. Separated fathers need to ensure there's a spare packet of pads in their bathroom cupboard, or in their briefcase. 'It's the degree of thoughtfulness and being able to talk about it naturally . . . a lot of girls think their dads don't know anything about it,' Bennett says.

Girls have mixed feelings about puberty. Many of them are more worried about the circumstances of their first period than the fact of its arrival. 'I don't want to stand up after class and everyone see I had my period for the first time,' one says. Kellie Lyneham, deputy principal (student wellbeing) at Korowa Anglican Girls' School, has a nine-year-old. Her daughter is excited about that phase of her life – something quite different from herself at the same age. Lyneham says her reading, as a mother, has made her think that as parents and educators we've been too focused on menstruation, not the stages leading up to it. 'I think we've been underestimating the impact of the developmental stage,' she says.

The body and the brain are intertwined, sending messages to each other, and just as a girl's body is going through significant and rapid change and growth, so too is her brain. Dr Hannah Kirk, a National Health and Medical Research Council (NHMRC) Early Career Research Fellow and a researcher at the Turner Institute for Brain and Mental Health at Monash University, is an expert on brain development. She says that the body–brain nexus is at the centre of understanding the development of a ten-year-old girl. In lay terms, brain development is a gradual and ongoing process that begins before birth and travels into adulthood. 'It's really in those first few years of life that we see the biggest changes in brain develop-ment – more than a million new neural connections are forming every second in the first few years of life, and after that period of really rapid creation, those connections tend to be reduced,' Dr Kirk says. That process is called pruning and it essentially allows our brains to become more efficient. We develop simple processes first, like vision and hearing, and they're built upon to form more complex skills, like language and cognition. As the brain matures, it becomes more specialised. A good example of this is language. When a child is first born, every language sounds the same to them. But a tuning process means they soon 'specialise' in the language they are hearing.

So where, at the age of ten, is the brain at? 'That is something that is very difficult to determine,' Dr Kirk says, 'because brain development is this dynamic process, it's not ever stopping. It's really difficult – impossible – to determine what percentage brain development has occurred by a certain age.' But by middle childhood – nine to eleven years – individuals will typically have well-honed language skills and cognitive abilities that allow them to gather information. These are skills like being able to focus their attention, or swap from one task to another, or not speak over each other, and even to hold information. 'They are the core cognitive skills that we call executive functions, and they're really integral for successful cognitive development,' Dr Kirk says. They're also crucial for school learning and emotional wellbeing. But at this age, judgement is not fully formed, and organisational and planning abilities are still growing. Understanding long-term consequences will take much longer. Huge variations exist between one child and the next, however, and can be attributable to genetics or environmental factors like stress, abuse, poverty and even maternal depression. Several times during this project, experts raised the examples of foster children, who often reach puberty early – almost as though their circumstances impel them to grow up. Bryan Smith, the executive director of Foster and Kinship Care in Queensland, has been a foster parent with his wife Linda for more than 150 children over 28 years. 'We've had children from as little as three days – parents going into detention and being deported – right through to children who were only going to be short-term and ended up here forever,' he says. And with the median age in care for children being between seven and twelve, that's included dozens of ten-year-old girls. 'Their bodies and their brains are telling them that they have to grow up early to protect themselves. That's part of their bodies' survival skills – and their survival skills,' he says. This means they often take on 'teenage concepts' years before they are ready. 'The things that you would expect at thirteen and fourteen, we are seeing at nine and ten.'

Professor Susan Sawyer from the University of Melbourne explains it this way: a child's brain is a brain that has its orientation towards the family, while an adolescent brain is one that becomes much more responsive to peer environments and is able to compare and contrast. 'Hence, as one passes through adolescence, why do we suddenly become interested in having the most trendy jeans or sneakers that we've never had any interest in before? Because we're able to compare and contrast in terms of status and therefore to judge our own position in the context of that,' she says. 'Now, ten-year-olds are still in the very earliest stages of that. It becomes heightened in the fourteen- to sixteen-years age group. But it is a period where there is a huge amount of activity taking place.'

Wildly different developmental milestones make parenting and educating teens a challenge. Sometimes children don't meet a milestone by the time 'labels' suggest they should; a year later, they might have forged ahead. 'That's all part of typical development and that's completely normal,' Dr Kirk says. But parenting has a real and measurable impact. 'We know things like high levels of parental involvement are associated with better performance on cognitive measures.' Inconsistency in things like parental discipline is associated with poorer performance. And crucially – and I'll visit a father's influence later – Dr Kirk says a father's involvement has a positive impact on children's cognitive skills.

So what about girls who struggle in class at ten – is that a window into difficulties in later years? No, says Dr Kirk. It might simply be delayed or late maturity. 'It's also important to remember that what is taught in schools is a very selective amount of skills. It does not cover everything. It's not covering the broad spectrum of abilities that children have. Children have a wide variety of strengths and weaknesses, and sometimes the education system is not able to capture those strengths, which obviously can have an impact on that feeling of self-esteem and self worth.'

So many times during this research, I have wished every ten-year-old girl could hear that.

3

Friends and foes

'Love yourself [and] genuinely and authentically
love others so that you are a friend relationship
magnet. Put down the device and have
fact-to-face contact more than screen.'

Year 5 teacher

Aisha just wants one good friend, someone to sit with
and talk to at lunch. 'I find it hard to make friends
because I am so worried about if they like me or not,' she
says. Francesca is equally anxious. 'I'm hard to talk to,'
she says. Mei can identify. For her, finding and keeping
friends is the toughest part about being ten. 'Some of
them turn out to be using you,' she says. 'Real friends are
hard to discover.' These concerns can often be exacerbated
when girls move from their primary school to a middle
or senior school at around this age. 'I find it hard to meet

anyone because I am new and everyone has known each other for a long time,' says Ruby. 'I feel like I don't fit in.' Alice is in a similar situation. 'I find it hard when people already have formed friendship groups,' she says. 'And my parents think that I find it easier than I do.' Aanya's concern is slightly different. 'It's easy to make friends but hard to find the perfect friend for life,' she says. Lily doesn't want to stand out. 'I like to stick in a big group at my school, and at home I never go out and play with others because of my anxiety.'

Why is friendship so difficult to navigate at ten? Why do so many of our girls not know how to make friends, or keep friends? Why do they want to find that best friend for life, at ten, and change so much of who they are, simply to fit in? How do we teach them not to exclude others, and to value kindness and forgiveness when one of their peers makes a mistake? And why is there so much drama – with girls and not boys – around friendship?

Those questions didn't begin as mine, and if there was a single issue that sat above others, where both girls and their parents struggled, this is it. 'Why do some girls become so unkind and nasty?' one mother asks. Another has a story to tell: 'Last year my daughter learnt the hard way that if you behave badly towards a friend and hurt their feelings then they may just walk away from the friendship instead of finding ways of forgiveness. The other parents told their daughter to walk away because "a good friend wouldn't behave that way" and that there would be no forgiveness for the mistake my daughter made. I found there is a lot of information available about walking way but not much about forgiveness and how it can play a role in healing friendships for our girls.' A third mother says, 'All she wants is to be loved, and I believe it's why she gets so frustrated and upset, because it doesn't come easily to her and she assumes reasons, like she has hairier legs or isn't pretty.' And this from a fourth mother: 'She is very worried and concerned about what others think, but I also think she is fairly intolerant of things herself and she is slow to forgive and forget.' From a fifth mother: 'She loves the idea of having friends but struggles to cross over from "being friendly" to actually being real friends.'

The problem for girls is not in recognising the attributes of a good friend but in cultivating and keeping friendships. The girls themselves put kindness as the number one characteristic they want in a ten-year-old buddy. That is to be celebrated. So too is the fact that they put 'being funny' strongly in second place. Together, those two qualities were mentioned by more than half of all ten-year olds. The third most common attribute ten-year-old girls nominate in a good friendship is wanting someone who is 'not a bully', or 'doesn't share rude things about you even if they're made up', or 'keeps a secret', or 'doesn't spread rumours'. Put those concerns under one umbrella and you have something close to what author and teens educator Rebecca Sparrow calls 'drama cyclones'. Sparrow says she spends weeks each year with this cohort, teaching them how to weather friendship storms. A few years ago she would have given the same talk to Year 9 girls.

Sparrow frequently delivers this example of how a drama cyclone unfolds. 'So it goes like this: you're at school and somebody ticks you off. Let's say they've been a bit of a jerk to you in the hallway or at the bag rack. If you then go into class and say to your friends, "XX is being a cow," you're actually creating a drama cyclone – you're turning it into a thing. And that's what you don't want. So your choices really are to let it go and accept that that person was in a bad mood just now, or you take the person aside and talk to them about it.' Perhaps out of a lack of confidence, an inability to articulate how they feel or the belief that there's safety in numbers, Sparrow reveals that the girl wronged will more often than not turn her friends against the bag-rack perpetrator, and what might have been bad or annoying behaviour, or even an accident, quickly turns into a diabolical incident that draws girls into taking sides, and sniggering, and converting others to 'their side'. It becomes a drama cyclone.

Friendship etiquette is a skill we need to teach our children, and many principals believe the need increased after the 2020 coronavirus lockdown, when girls didn't have regular physical interaction with their peers. Today, all too often, tech-savvy children reach for a phone or an iPad or school computer and send off a message that starts a chain reaction. Or they whisper about the person who wronged them to a friend in 'their' group, and a thread of outrage builds between classes and blankets them by lunchtime. Simple annoyances become friendship deciders. One of the most common examples comes about as a consequence of a girl sending a text to a friend at night. The sender sees the Read Receipt, but doesn't receive a reply. By morning, a 'drama cyclone' has developed and everyone knows it. The ten-year-old whose parents stopped her replying, or who read the message just before nodding off to sleep, is unfriended and ostracised. In the parlance of our ten-year-olds, she was responsible for her friend being 'left on read'.

Avoiding those drama cyclones should sit at the top of any friendship tips list we give our girls. So should an understanding of the fact that friendships are developed over time, and that we don't 'own' friends. Girls need to be encouraged to allow peers to move between groups, and to have the courage to do that themselves. We as parents don't befriend every person we meet, and girls need to understand that. They don't need to be friends with everyone in their cohort, but they need be friendly – and understand that difference. Along the way, they will make mistakes and need reminding that the kindness and forgiveness they seek in others ought to reside in them too. Is the friendship bigger than the mistake made? Brisbane

Girls Grammar School psychologist Tara McLachlan says setting boundaries is a crucial part of developing friendships, and girls need to learn to understand and explain their own 'line in the sand' to others. But it's a lesson girls struggle with. 'They just want to please and be liked,' McLachlan explains. 'They want to fit in, so they won't set those boundaries with friends.' The tone of a friendship is set early on, and if boundaries aren't part of that, one friend can take advantage of the other quickly, resulting in a power imbalance. 'It's then really hard to set that boundary later on,' says McLachlan. 'I feel like this is a life skill that's really, really important.'

Author Brené Brown talks about marble jar friends – a great analogy to share with ten-year-olds on how to learn to trust. The marble jar was used by Brown's daughter's teacher as a reward and discipline system. Each time the class did something positive, marbles were added to the jar and a celebration held each time they reached the brim. Marbles were removed for bad behaviour. But when Brené Brown's third-grade daughter came home, heartbroken, after friends broke her trust, she told her this: 'Trust is like a marble jar.' You share hard stories with certain friends because 'they've done thing after thing after thing where you're like, "I know I can share this with this person".'[1]

Principal Toni Riordan says the reason why the age of ten is so significant for friendships is that, up until that age, a girl's world has largely revolved around her home, her parents, her siblings and her pets. But at ten she becomes more outward-looking, and 'friendships really start to count'. Girls are looking for others who will match the love they have for family, and tensions will inevitably arise. 'Fitting in' is the verb I most frequently heard during this project, and friendship is the challenge ten-year-olds nominate as their most difficult. 'Sometimes I feel like I don't fit in with my friends, but I don't know why,' Rose told me. 'I don't fit in because my friends have changed,' Jenny says. Six other girls are in the same room as Rose and Jenny. Everyone nods. 'My friends liked me last year but now they're too cool for me, so I don't know what to do,' one says. Another says, 'I think it's because I'm tall, and that makes me feel like an outsider.' Another girl says, 'Friendship is really hard. I was sitting with a new group and I'm shy so they thought I didn't like them, and then the bossy girl told me to leave the group.'

Earlier, I made the point that ten-year-olds are not a homogeneous bunch and the colossal differences in development can impact on any class of this age. Many of their challenges are similar, and friendship stands out as one of those. But some girls also are able to find buddies with remarkable ease. 'I'm funny so it's easy,' one says. 'It's pretty easy because I think I have a winning personality,' another says. And my personal favourite: 'Very easy. It's almost like I'm a friend magnet.' But most – a big majority

– say friendship, on some days, is a mountain they have to climb. It exhausts them, and they don't know where to turn for help. Many schools boast social-emotional learning programs or socialisation programs to provide explicit strategies to help girls navigate friendships. They pair children up and encourage them to talk directly to each other, and provide expert speakers to address them on everything from the value of friendship to the importance of empathy in creating social bonds.

Catherine O'Kane, principal of Brisbane's All Hallows' School, says the way *we* communicated as children is in stark contrast to the way our daughters communicate. 'Kids were socialised, face to face; hours of playtime were spent with others and learning how to be with others,' she says. Like her peers in education, it doesn't take long for the discussion to turn to the suffocating influence of the smartphone. Many ten-year-olds, as babies, were given digital devices as 'pacifiers' and a consequence of that is now being seen in the struggle they have to respond appropriately to others, and even to understand visual clues. 'I think that for schools, the role there is some really intensive work in socialising, in making sure that ten-year-olds actually can work with each other, can be with each other,' O'Kane says. 'That becomes so important because it impacts on friendships, and on reading the social cues.' The role of parents is crucial. 'They have to be really wise about screen time,' says O'Kane. 'There have to be limits put on it. I'm not saying that children shouldn't have screen time – of course they should; it's part of everybody's life these days – but they have to be careful, and if you're going to give your child a smartphone, you have to help them be smart. Sometimes that means parental controls, because they are ten. Or say "no".' I couldn't find a single expert on ten-year-old girls who disagrees.

While our girls boast so many positive attributes that were not part of our childhood armoury, persistence and patience are increasingly being seen as old-fashioned or even irrelevant. The expectation of instant gratification is ubiquitous. This is demonstrated in the way in which children consider friendship. Most of them believe it should be achieved with the speed used to make a chocolate milkshake; that it should only take a chat at morning tea, or sitting next to someone on a bus ride home, for a friendship to be created. But that's rarely true of deep or life-long friendships, which, like flowers, need to be nurtured and watered and helped through challenges. Some girls will find a best friend at school; others might need to wait for years. But it's the end result – that invaluable bond where no secret is too big or too small, and where a warm embrace works wonders – that's important. Often it is built up over joint interests and values. Principal Toni Riordan met her oldest friend Kathy on her first day at university. Despite growing up in the same town, they had not previously met. They both loved reading and music, and their values mirrored each other's. 'I just knew she was kind, interested and intelligent, an outward-looking person,' Riordan says. She was almost a decade older than ten, but the friendship endures.

But even if a 'best friend' appears at school, our girls still need other friends – both inside and outside of school. There needs to be a ceiling on Instagram followers, not friendships. Toni Riordan says she sometimes wonders if our daughters look for a best friend in a bid to value themselves more. The 'obsession' with having one best friend starts in Years 4 and 5, sometimes earlier, and often creates havoc. 'I think when you drill down into that, they're looking for trust, and someone to have their back,' Rebecca Sparrow says. But she warns against groups of three. 'A group of three means there are two established best friends and the third person is put on a shelf when they are not wanted. "Oh, we'll play with you today. Oh no, we just want it to be the two of us now." The ground shifts all the time. It's very rare to have a three that isn't problematic. I mean, if you've got one, great, but I would say you are better off having [a] four,' she says. Author Phyllis Fagell says ten-year-olds are very aware of where they sit in friendship groups. 'They'll be able to tell you, down to the nth degree, what the order of popularity ranking is by ten,' she says. 'They will know who is top and who is bottom, and every rung in between. They're highly attuned to where they fit in that hierarchy and who that means they're supposed to be hanging out with.' Helen Adams, head of junior school at St Mary's Anglican Girls' School in Perth, says boys 'do friendships better than girls', and this point is telling. 'They've got their friends they go surfing with and they've got their friends they play rugby with, and I'm not going to ask a friend who plays rugby to go surfing because I know he doesn't like it, and he won't get bitter and twisted about it, whereas many girls have this "I should be invited and if I'm not that's a real slight on me" attitude.' This difference between boys and girls was pointed out to me several times, and is perhaps the reason why some girls, at ten, hang onto the uncomplicated bonds they have with their male peers as long as they can. There's less drama and more playing.

In the journey through school, all children will make mistakes. They will hurt someone's feelings, betray a friend, or stand back and ignore bad behaviour. Learning from that is part of growing up, but it is also part of developing deep and meaningful friendships. This is where those boundaries, raised by school counsellor Tara McLachlan, are so important. A short conversation between girls, while difficult, can ward off heartbreak for everyone. Girls need to have the courage to take aside the person who wronged them and explain their unhappiness. This is a skill, like learning to stand up and address a class, or play an instrument. It needs to be practised and role-played. And that's where we, as parents, can be invaluable. 'We say to our kids, "just say no", or, "just do this", expecting that they're going to have the language or the words,' Rebecca Sparrow says. 'They don't. They're nine and ten!' They need role-play at home, to practise phrases and learn to use them in those tricky moments, she says.

Children learn from their parents. For example, the more parents gossip in front of their daughters, the more likely their daughters are to do the same. Paul Dillon, the director and founder of Drug and Alcohol Research and Training Australia (DARTA), says research provides evidence that children are taking on the lessons delivered by their parents between the ages of three and eight. Those lessons might relate to alcohol consumption or how to be treated in a relationship, or even how to get whatever you want. Friendship is no different: role-modelling works.

One issue that popped up here, repeatedly, was the attribution of labels – by parents, describing their daughters' role in friendship groups.

'I call mine a social observer.'

'Mine's the peacemaker.'

'I have a messenger; she runs messages from group to group.'

'She's the queen bee, and everyone wants part of her. That's not fair.'

'I don't know why, but I think mine might be a mean girl.'

And so it went on. A goody-two shoes. The quiet one. The shy one. The third wheel. The boss. The bright spark. The best keeper of secrets.

Children learn to be the label they are given, and so many ten-year-olds see themselves playing a specific role in their friendship group. 'When we label kids, kids will lean into that label,' says Karen Young, founder of *Hey Sigmund*, a popular website which addresses children's mental health and attracts millions of readers each year. 'If it is something that they think fits them even a little bit, they will lean into that,' she says. 'The other thing is that kids live up or down to our expectations, and once there's a label there, it can be heard as an expectation. So, if you're a people pleaser, there's an expectation that "I won't argue" or "I won't mind".' That can carry a lot of influence as our girls develop. 'So a people pleaser in a group is going to please the group. Sometimes that will be a strength; sometimes they will come across as kind and easygoing. But it's about the flexibility between the two. You want them also to be able to speak their own mind,' Young says.

Helen Adams says it is important for parents not to hold onto feelings on behalf of their daughters. Like others in her role, she sees girls moving on from friend-ship rows, but parents – particularly mothers – struggling to do that. 'I also lay a lot of blame at the foot of what these girls watch on social media and also the TV shows they watch,' she says. She's right. The friendships are wrapped up, often, in cattiness. Disputes are nasty. Bonds are not cherished and celebrated. That, coupled with their parents' involvement in school arguments (and that can be common), can make it more difficult for girls. Another head of junior school says she has seen 'an escalation' in this in recent years. 'It's a catastrophe if they're told their little one in kindy has been told that "you're not my friend today". Little girls will do this and they don't have the sophistication of language to actually say: "I don't want to play that game". Their immediate response is "I'm not your friend". Parents tend to catastrophise that. They hold onto it.' And that learnt behaviour continues into primary school.

Phyllis Fagell says parents need to find a way to become part of their child's support crew, and need to consider language, timing and location in the delivery of this support. She tells the story of a therapist whose daughter seemed to 'shut down' when she really needed support. The therapist 'was doing everything she could to help her child. She'd say, "What did you learn today?" and the kid would really bristle. She thought she was doing everything right: she had the poker face; she didn't react; she was giving emotional distance. And then one day she changed the question just a little bit and said, "What did your teacher teach you?" And she got an answer.' The lesson here is that in parenting a ten-year-old girl one needs to consider her state of mind – for example, how her day played out. 'So when they get in the car after school and you want to hear all about their day, they may need to go into a dark closet by themselves,' Fagell says. Perhaps that state of mind is not too far removed from us, their parents, after a hard day at the office.

Without doubt, for many girls anxiety plays a role in friendship. Take this honest and thoughtful assessment from one mother, about her daughter. 'She always wants to dictate how the "play" goes, and when others get sick of following her lead she is unwilling to change and her relationships suffer because of this. I am worried that she'll have no friends.' That was not an uncommon concern. Karen Young says while anxiety can lead a girl to empathy – an understanding of isolation or being left out – it can also 'drive a need to control, and not in a horrible dominating sense'. She says anxious children will sometimes want to be in charge of the play, and the players. 'And that can cause problems in friendship groups, because they will want everything to go their way. That is not because they want power. It's about having safety.'

It was a simple request from one mother that took me to the office of Associate Professor Kate Williams from the Queensland University of Technology. 'If there could be a part of your book that addresses tweens with special needs (autism) and how these girls really deserve to have the same opportunities at friendship, and how these friendships can really benefit the typical girl, that would be my dream come true,' the mother wrote. Williams, an early childhood expert, has heard this before. She says that problems here are often exacerbated by the fact that cases of high-functioning Autism Spectrum Disorder (ASD) and Attention Deficit Hyperactivity Disorder (ADHD) tend to be undiagnosed and under-recognised in girls. There was also a rare divergence here between educators and those who sat outside the school system. 'Schools have to step up here,' one senior researcher in girls' development says. 'Some schools have gone down this road of being too concerned about their marketing brochures and academic scores. They need to step up with their mental health.' Her point is that our children all have challenges – they can't be exceptional at everything – and we should talk about that more. We should make girls look outside themselves, to be kind, and to make sure we as parents and educators practise what we preach. One expert in teenage development, who advises schools, tells the story of a parent's response to finding out her daughter was in the B netball team, not the A team. She recalls hearing the mother say, '"I don't want my girl on that team with those retards."

When you have that mentality, you are less open to your child being friends with kids who are different.'

It is also antithetical to what we are told determines who later becomes a leader in life: a person who can take others with her, who will listen more than she will talk, who seeks the wisdom of others and who 'leads from the front'. Every expert on the future of work encourages the development of these ironically labelled 'soft skills'. And every educator is united in believing that our daughters benefit from valuing the connection and warmth and kindness that comes from genuine inclusion and friendship.

4

Smartphones and social media

'My big message to parents is you've got to be
the pilot not the passenger of the digital plane.'

Dr Kristy Goodwin, child and technology expert

The girl is about eleven, and undercover police video identification teams have so far not been able to find her. But her face, and what she does, haunts them. From the video they've seen, it's obvious that she's distraught. 'She knows what's about to happen to her because it's happened so many times before with this individual,' Detective Inspector Jon Rouse says. 'He makes her do humiliating things to herself in her own house.'

Jon Rouse is the manager of covert online, victims' identification and training at the Australian Centre to Counter Child Exploitation (ACCCE). He's also a father.

'I'm fortunate my daughter's twenty-five now and she's escaped all of this,' he says. 'But this is just horrendous. She's somebody's daughter, and has probably come out of her bedroom with tears in her eyes and Mum and Dad probably went, "What's wrong?", thinking that she's just had a fight with a friend or a bust-up or something, when in fact I know what she's just done to herself. I saw the threats that he wrote to her in the message, calling her a good slave and all of this kind of thing. God, how does a kid deal with that?'

The teams working under Detective Inspector Rouse are highly trained. They pick up material as it circulates the globe on the dark net or through digital seizures. It's encrypted, and it takes months, sometimes years, of painstaking work to bring a perpetrator to justice. But finding the victims can be even harder. Clues like accents help, but officers use anything they can see in the online footage to try to track down and remove a child from harm. It might be the curtain in the room where the offence takes place, or the type of floorboard. If they're lucky, they might get a glimpse of a piece of architecture which will allow them to work with peers across the world to narrow down the country, the state, the city, the street and then the home where a young girl's bedroom has become her prison.

How does a ten- or eleven-year-old get caught up in such a hideous crime? In this case, as in many, the perpetrator has 'procured' his victim on a social media platform before moving her across to Skype. But it could be any of a dozen or more communication methods; he just needs to see her, and be able to give her orders. She might think she's talking to a thirteen-year-old boy from the next suburb, or a girl she's met briefly. Predators are clever in choosing their prey, and grooming them. Perhaps they will befriend her over weeks, or months, before offering all sorts of inducements – from movie tickets to money to meeting her favourite movie star. All she has to do is remove her top, this once. And then he's got her. 'Once he's taken that one photograph, or she's done that one thing that he asked her to do . . . then he has the power,' Rouse says. The sex predator will capture the photo or video and save it. And then he will use it to 'sextort' the child: he will threaten to send it to all her friends and put it online across the globe, and send a copy to her mum and dad – unless she does it again. Or goes further.

Most children don't fall prey to this sort of activity, but it is too common, experts say. Some girls will send a nude selfie of themselves to a boy who says he's interested – and with this happening at ages eleven and twelve, many, many schools in Australia are dealing with the fallout of that. And a plea from principals here: don't automatically think it will never be your daughter. Some girls will have two social media accounts on their phone: one where Mum and Dad are friends, and another secret account. The smartphone will become the means of round-the-clock connectivity and, unchecked, that can carry them into a world of bullying and social exclusion. It can also dominate their sleep patterns, affect academic or sporting results, determine their friendships and, most importantly, determine how they see themselves.

Of course, smartphones and social media have revolutionised their lives for good, too. The smartphone can serve as an asset to their education, providing knowledge at their fingertips. It can feed their passion for cooking and sport and reading. It can provide security. It can allow instant contact with parents. These things are a given. But smartphones and social media present two big new challenges that we need to understand.

Jon Rouse's job is made more difficult by these two giants. The first is the ready availability of any number of attractive social media apps marketed specifically to young children; the second is their access to celebrities online. In the ten-year-old milieu, celebrities are compelling figures. Children are attracted to them. They want to mirror what they look like, what they wear, what they eat and they desperately want to meet them. Perpetrators of online abuse will pick up on a child's infatuation with a star and trick them into believing they know them personally, and could even arrange a meeting – if only the child does what the perpetrator asks. If they take off their top, just once, the perpetrator might promise that next time the celebrity is in their area, the ten-year-old could meet them. 'What it means,' says Rouse, 'is that a child with a mobile device – whether it be an iPad, iPhone or whatever – and in the safety and sanctity of their own home, is producing child-abuse material.' In the case at the outset of this chapter, the predator sent the increasingly disgusting 'self-produced' material from the girl to his child sex offender networks. Predators like to share this content – that's their modus operandi.

I know the answer to my next question before I ask it. What worries Jon Rouse most about this particular case? Rouse's voice drops, and you can hear the father as much as the international crime fighter in his response. 'I wonder if that little girl has got to the point where she's taken her life, because I know that that happens. That's the worst possible scenario.' He's thinking of Amanda Todd, a Canadian teenager who suicided after posting a video in which she explained how she'd been blackmailed into exposing her breasts via webcam.

Children simply aren't capable of dealing with a predator's behaviour or the fallout from the abuse. Which is why, Rouse emphasises, 'education and awareness of parents and carers and guardians is critical. They need to understand that this is going on.' Investigators recognise why girls struggle to tell their parents, or others, that they're in trouble. They're ashamed, they think they've done something wrong and they have a threat hanging over their heads – if they reveal the dirty secret, the whole world will know. 'Mum and Dad,' Rouse pleads, 'sit down with your kid and go through their phone, and have a look at the applications that they're using.' And importantly, 'Drop [the image of convicted paedophile] Dennis Ferguson from your radar okay, because that's not what all predators look like.' Predators are young, and old. They come from all walks of life, and boast all sorts of qualifications and occupations. 'You cannot put them into a box and say, "stay away from that".'

In my research I observed a gulf between the concerns of parents and those of law enforcement over the use of social media. Of course, parents express concern about their child's social media use, whether they are accessing it on their own phone or a friend's device. But their concern didn't top parental worries, and when it did, it fell well short of the ugly world Jon Rouse describes.

These are typical concerns of mothers of tween girls:

'I don't want her meeting boys via online resources and not experiencing sexual encounters and dating in a beautiful traditional order, i.e. hanging out with groups of girls and boys, holding hands, kissing, then other

sexual activities before sex, that take place over months and years.'

'Exposure to over-sexualised stuff in media and a willingness to please others that may go against her better judgement.'

'What concerns me is the possible creeping influence over the next few years of friends who have unfettered access to all the crap online, parents who put zero restrictions on smartphones and then this info becomes too much too early.'

'Social media when it arrives like a hurricane into their lives. How do I protect her self-esteem in this kind of world?'

'I worry about the quality and quantity of the porn saturating young boys' viewing and wish that she is never subjected to their unrealistic and misogynistic views of early sexual experiences.'

'The premature sexualisation of young girls worries me greatly. Of course that's linked to social media, body image, female representation in all forms of media, and could lead you down the rabbit hole.'

A few girls have picked up the message that social media isn't all good.

'I'm on none because I don't like people or things that will sell my information.'

'No way. I'm not on social media. It's dangerous.'

But these girls were the exception. About half of the 1600 mothers consulted said their child had a smartphone, and most felt justified in the provision of it. The reasons varied: it allows a child to communicate freely with both parents in a separated family; it assists parents in navigating school pick-ups; it provides security for children with medical challenges, like anaphylaxis, asthma and anxiety; it is a step towards providing and encouraging greater independence. As noted earlier, COVID-19, which forced our daughters out of the playground and into their homes, away from friends, saw a surge in smartphone ownership by ten-year-olds. Appreciation of the phone as an instrument of social connection explained why parents wrapped up a smartphone and handed it to their daughter as a tenth birthday present.

'It is a lifeline to her friends, who all have them.'

'She got her first one for her birthday a month ago. It was important because she wanted to be more independent.'

'Yes, it was a gift for her birthday just before this virus situation hit. I want her to be able to contact me if she

is on a play date, or if I'm running late. She talks to her friends and stays in touch with her world.'

'Her friendship group is really important to her wellbeing and has helped her during COVID.'

'I struggle with the enormity of the world of a smartphone but also like fostering independence, trust and awareness for her.'

'Yes. She was given a phone at the start of this year because she changed schools. She gets anxious and it helps her remain calm when she can contact me.'

'We have a relationship based on trust and communication. I know she will use it wisely and it's a useful and fun tool.'

Those who chose not to provide their child with a phone never cited 'grooming' or the threat of cyberbullying as their reasons. Almost unanimously, denial of a smartphone was motivated by a plan to keep their child a child, and delay social media use until their self-regulation skills were better honed.

'I think smartphones can be really destructive if they are too young to self-regulate, and she won't be getting one until high school.'

'She does not need access to any more of the world than she already has. We feel being a kid for as long as possible is sacred.'

'I teach teenagers and it cemented my opinion of her not needing one.'

For those parents who had decided to stand their ground, the pressure they felt was immense. Many were concerned what the impact of their child not having a smartphone might be, when so many of their friends did.

'All of her friends already have phones. I'm not one for giving them something just because everyone has it, but it can get to a point that I feel I am leaving them out of things and it affects too much.'

'There is massive pressure. She is the last of her friends to have a mobile [and TikTok].'

Regret was already evident in the households of some of those who'd granted access early.

'She likes to use it to FaceTime her friends, which is good while we are in lockdown. I regret letting her have it during normal times.'

'Yes. I regret giving her one.'

'Yes. We always clash about it because of the amount of time she spends on her phone.'

The smartphone–social media issue is a tricky one for parents because of how it plays out in friendships circles. At lunchtime, and waiting for the bus, there are those who have a smartphone and those who don't, those who are able to contact their friends online and those who can't. And certainly that can make it difficult for a ten-year-old taking the first tentative steps towards independence. But the journey of those *with* them can be even trickier. Removing a device is more difficult than refusing it in the first place. And once it's given, many parents are then pressured to allow access to social media platforms, particularly TikTok and Instagram. Often that decision is made by what platforms other children are on. 'I'm on Snapchat, TikTok, Whatsapp for family and relatives and Hangout for friends, Instagram and YouTube,' one girl says. Dozens of others said the same. Parents openly admit the struggle here, and COVID certainly played a part in many parents' decision to relax restrictions in relation to both the number and type of apps allowed.

The social media apps named by ten-year-olds as their preferred options were TikTok and Instagram, but many, many children also boasted accounts with Snapchat and Houseparty. WhatsApp, Pinterest, Messenger, FaceTime and Minecraft were also popular. YouTube, WeChat and Messenger Kids were also raised by children. The pressure to keep up with the child at the next desk is a constant. While children who are not yet the owners of a smartphone are often able to access social media via other technology, particularly an iPad or a computer, the kudos and convenience of a smartphone means that a child who doesn't have one can feel left out in the cold.

'All my friends have a phone and TikTok. I'm the ONLY one who doesn't have it. It's not fair.'

'I keep asking. What age do you think I should be able to get it?'

'Soon I won't have any friends because my whole group is on TikTok and Instagram. I am always left out.'

Parents feel that pressure.

'TikTok is a great pastime and way for children to connect with their peers. But the music and dances are often sexually suggestive without them realising. I worry we are unknowingly grooming our children.'

'My daughter can get really persistent online with her friends and has difficulty when she doesn't get immediate responses. She needs that constant reassurance from her friends online. She also has major FOMO.'

'There is [pressure] from other parents who don't understand why my daughter doesn't have her own phone and social media. A phone will be allowed in Year 6. My daughter is allowed TikTok on her iPad.'

'She was constantly going behind our backs to download it no matter what parental controls we put on. We eventually decided to allow her as it's almost impossible to police.'

'A lot of her friends have Insta and Snapchat already. She already has TikTok, which I know is just as bad, and I wish I didn't allow it but don't think I could have held off much longer.'

'There is a HUGE amount of pressure around social media. She has TikTok, which I was wary of to begin with. Most of her friends also have Snapchat, Instagram, etc.'

'Soooo much pressure. TikTok was allowed at eleven for our eldest and we were waiting until ten for our nine-year-old, but caved due to COVID.'

'I allowed it [TikTok] after six months of begging. I caved to the pressure of her being the only one who doesn't have it.'

'Socially your child is disadvantaged if they are not [on social media]. I let my eleven-year-old have TikTok and Snapchat younger than I thought. This was mainly *because she switched schools at Year 5 and would be literally one of the only ones in her year group that wasn't on it. So much of the communication is done via this that I'd feel bad for sidelining my daughter. My nine-year-old is on TikTok and Snapchat ...'*

Read those comments to cyber-safety expert and author Susan McLean and you can hear her shudder. Messenger Kids, she says, is the only app a child under the age of thirteen is permitted to use, and if a child is on others, they are breaking the law. 'This does my head in,' says McLean, 'because it's a parent complicit in helping their child to lie. There is no other polite way to put it. The parent is condoning lying by saying "yes, my child is thirteen".' The scope for predators, on platforms where children are able to interact or dance or communicate, is enormous. McLean, a former Victorian police officer who now regularly attends schools to talk about cyber safety, rattles off examples of cases where data on children has been gathered and sold, and where biometric facial recognition has been used to identify children. 'I've dealt personally with lots of kids who have been groomed on Instagram. So again, I'm not saying a thirteen-year-old is not going to be groomed, or a fourteen-year-old. What I'm saying is, I should never have to deal with an eight-year-old girl who has been groomed on Instagram, because she should not have been there in the first place,' she says. The surge in online problems centred on both cyberbullying (dealt with in the next chapter) and child grooming. Indeed, the Internet Watch Foundation – a UK charity that finds and removes images of children subject to sex abuse online – says it and its partners blocked more than 8.8 million attempts by UK internet users to access videos and images of children suffering sexual abuse. And that was during the initial COVID-19 lockdown alone![1] One-third of all child-abuse material found has been posted by children themselves, and more than three-quarters of this features eleven- to thirteen-year-old children, mostly girls.[2]

Susan McLean says that she's been made aware of cases in Australia involving girls as young as eight. 'Before having a smartphone, there was no opportunity for that child to be groomed or to strip naked on a webcam. But now they have the opportunity. And paedophiles aren't dumb: it's much easier to suck a ten-year-old into doing something than it is a sixteen-year-old.'

Parents are culpable, but so too, it seems, are schools. The coronavirus pandemic lockdowns in Australia saw schools begin using online learning. Susan McLean says there is now a parallel increase in bullying, social isolation and other problems, and she believes some schools have encouraged that by asking students to upload dance and physical education participation. Some teachers thought it was a 'cool' way to engage children. One school set up every student with the same password to access their Google accounts. At another school, a teacher photographed students then posted it to her personal social media account. McLean says the increased use of social media will impact on our girls' mental health, and we can expect both musculoskeletal issues and eye problems, as young children use their mobile phones in bed, hunched over on the lounge or while walking. 'You will see a massive digital footprint of these children that is out there forever,' McLean says. During lockdown she says she was writing upwards of twenty emails every couple of days to principals, saying, 'What the hell are your teachers on?'

This is not just about smartphones but access to social media. According to the Australian Bureau of Statistics in 2018, 97 per cent of households with children aged under fifteen had access to the internet.[3] The average age now for a girl to see pornography online – accidentally or on purpose – is just eleven. It's about this age, also, that schools begin to grapple with girls sending nude 'selfies'. When Susan McLean visits schools, she starts one of her activities by finding out how many children are on what platforms. 'And they're very honest with me. I would have probably 80 per cent of Grade 5s and 6s on one or more social media sites that they shouldn't be on, and in Grades 3 and 4 – which is the age we are talking about – it would be about 75 per cent of any school that I visit anywhere in the world,' she says.

My interview with child and technology expert Dr Kristy Goodwin is at 5:30 am, and before speaking to me she's already checked her emails. 'I have three or four emails that are awful,' she says. 'The content is distressing – all from parents whose young daughters had seen inappropriate content online and two of them had awful encounters with cyberbullying.' Her advice to parents is twofold: to delay introduction, and to start to establish boundaries early. She says she's yet to find a parent who regrets holding off on giving their child a smartphone. 'What I find when I work with schools is that the kids all dupe their parents, saying, "Such-and-such has one", "This person has this app". And when the parents dig a little deeper, they'll find that's not the truth. And they all wish they hadn't given them one.' While research looking at links between mental health and social media were 'conflicting and contradictory', Dr Goodwin worries about the 'displacement effect': the opportunity cost of what children are missing out on while attached to their devices. Children are missing out now on basic and critical needs, like their relationship with others, good sleep and physical movement.

We are now also seeing a young generation of parents – mothers and fathers – who have their own close relationships with their phones. And that's led, in some cases, to something termed 'digital abandonment', or 'technoglect'. 'It's a real phenomenon,' Dr Goodwin says. Some parents' addiction to social media has been behind complaints to authorities from children, including several relating to missing out on dinner 'because Mum is on her phone'. No expert dismisses the alluring nature of social media; Dr Goodwin labels it a 'state of insufficiency' – the idea that the online world is a bottomless bowl. 'There is never a sense of being done or being complete. There's always another social media feed I can look through,' she says.

Given a magic wand to change anything for our girls, Lisa Miller, the head of junior school at Melbourne's Strathcona Girls Grammar, would target social media. 'I would make all social media illegal until they are thirteen, and there needs to be some consequences for parents who let their children do it. Allow them to be little girls. Allow them to play,' she says. Miller has a tween daughter herself, and can see the defining nature social media has in the school grounds. 'They're certainly exposed to a lot more through social media. I think, in this age group, there's a shift in behaviour where they're not mentally ready or developed to deal with those platforms and you see this shift in behaviour. And the other girls who aren't necessarily on those platforms then find it quite confusing.'

That 'teenage-type behaviour' can see the girls begin to dance more provocatively, for example, without any genuine understanding of what it might represent. Miller, along with many others, also raises the issue of its impact on friendships. 'They're the new cool, popular kids, and they can have quite a control over other girls because they realise "I have access to this and you don't". The other girls who are just generally being nine- and ten-year-olds get quite confused and can't quite understand that relationship and how it's forming, because girls at that age still want to be playing outside and being kids, and playing make-believe.' She agrees schools need to work on this, as well as parents. 'Schools need to make space for that; allow them to not be so crowded by curriculum and having to learn things by a certain age. They get there in the end.'

Parents, too, need to safeguard their children's childhoods. McLean says parents need to 'find their own tribe' – others with a similar ethos – and work together. 'You pick your fights. Is it worth fighting over a messy bedroom? Probably not, because no child ever died from having a messy bedroom. But certainly we know when physical and mental health and safety is at risk – which it is when they are using technology – that is a fight worth having.' Many parents were genuinely frightened of saying 'no', she says. 'The day before school started this year, I got a call from a mum. "I wonder if you could help me," she said. "I'm a bit concerned about my six-year-old son, who's been playing computer games for about twelve hours a day over the holidays, every day, and I'm a bit worried that he might not fit back into school tomorrow." And when I said, "Well, at this point you really need to disconnect the internet," she said, "Oh I tried that, but I can't bear to look at his sad little face."' McLean says parents should remember that social media offers its users a 'very adult world'. 'And we're giving it to a ten-year-old. Parents wouldn't dump their kids in Pitt Street Mall in Sydney, or Queen Street Mall in Brisbane, at 2 am and say, "Go have fun, find some new friends and come home when you're ready." So why are you doing it online?'

Jon Rouse understands parents wanting to provide their child with a phone, especially to allow contact. He also understands the pressure they are under to do so. But there's one thing he wants parents to know, and that is that they need to educate themselves and know the dangers of the device. 'They're displaying an enormous level of naivety if they don't think this [child grooming] is happening in Australia, and if they don't think that their child is potentially vulnerable to this. I'm sure that there's mums and dads out there who take an inordinate amount of interest in their children's safety. But the evidence for us is that there's probably a greater number of parents who don't take that level of interest. Please sit down and stop being their friend. You have a right to inspect that phone, you have a right to have password access to that phone. Don't think you're violating your child's privacy. You're actually being a parent by doing that.'

Bullying, online and off

'I wish I knew when I was [a child] what I know now,
because when those kids said things or did things,
I would always question myself, I would rarely
question them. But I know now . . . I was right.'

Ros Curtis, principal, St Margaret's Anglian Girls School

Bron had just received a smartphone but wasn't allowed social media. That didn't stop a boy she knew – a family friend – asking, via WhatsApp, for a nude photo. She told him to go away and leave her alone. He badgered her. When that didn't work, he sent a photoshopped image of her head on somebody else's naked body. 'He continued with the badgering,' Dr Kristy Goodwin, an expert in children and technology, says. 'She was just about to turn her phone off and then came a video of him self-harming – with a threat that if she didn't send through the real material he would follow through with his attempt.'

How does a tween girl deal with that? Bron's next step was understandable. She snapped a photo of her breasts, without her head, in an attempt to alleviate the situation that was unfolding. What happened next was as predictable as it was lamentable. As Dr Goodwin tells it, 'He took a screen shot of the photo. You could see the phone number.' And he distributed that on a whole range of social media platforms.

One case, from one expert. This book could be filled with dozens of others. When cyber-safety expert Susan McLean visits schools, she asks children what cyberbullying means. It's a good question, because the boundaries between 'being mean' and cyberbullying are indistinct. Of course, sometimes it's frighteningly clear to both children and adults what cyberbullying means. 'I had this little girl – she was ten – at a Catholic primary school in Melbourne,' says McLean. 'Her answer was, "It's when someone tells you to kill yourself online."' If any of us think that is a one-off answer, we're wrong.

There is no single, Australia-wide definition of what cyberbullying is. Australia's eSafety Commissioner defines it as behaviour that may include abusive texts and emails, hurtful messages, images or videos, excluding or humiliating others and spreading nasty online gossip, or creating fake accounts to trick someone or humiliate them.[1] In 2018

I chaired the Queensland Anti-Cyberbullying Taskforce, set up after fourteen-year-old Amy 'Dolly' Everett took her own life as a consequence of bullying. We determined that bullying was behaviour that intended to harm, was usually repeated, and often involved misuse of power.[2] That imbalance of power is important: it distinguishes bullying from classroom nastiness or meanness. And to deal with cyberbullying properly, it's worth our children knowing the difference.

At school, as in life, there will always be people who want to put someone else down. In Years 5 and 6, that might present as someone telling a girl she's hopeless at Art, or won't make the top netball team. That's not bullying. Girls need to navigate those put-downs and not judge themselves as others might judge them. That's a skill they need to develop, because they will encounter people like that everywhere: at school, while undertaking extracurricular activities and once they join the workforce. Bullying begins when an imbalance of power presents itself and someone feels threatened or intimidated. Rebecca Sparrow, who answers anonymous questions from tween and teen girls in her *Ask Me Anything* podcast, gives an example from when she was in Year 7. Each day she'd walk to her bus stop and the same boy would be there. "'Bye, Rubella," he would say. He thought it was hilarious to call me Rubella.' Sparrow asks ten-year-old girls whether the boy was a bully. 'And they'd say, "Yes, he was trying to hurt your feelings and it was repeated, so yes, it is." And I'd say, "No, it's not." I thought he was a complete moron. I couldn't care less. I'd look at him and say, "Shut up, Andrew."' Her point is that there wasn't an imbalance of power; Andrew was more jerk than bully. 'Now if Andrew had been with other boys, that would be different. Or if he'd been in an older grade, that would be different.' That's because it would have introduced an imbalance of power. Sparrow, who now has a daughter who is eleven, says she wouldn't go back to that age for all the money in the world. 'And I think that's why, when our kids come home and they talk about feeling stressed about school or that it's difficult, we need to have enormous empathy for that, because there's behaviour we expect our kids to put up with that we would never put up with in a workplace. Never.'

So how common is bullying online? Experts say at least one in five young people reports being socially excluded, threatened or abused online. According to the eSafety Commissioner, almost 30 per cent sought help from their friends. The good news is that 55 per cent sought help from their parents.[3] In those instances, it's crucial for parents to really listen to what their daughter is saying. That allows her to open up, but it also ensures you know whether someone has been mean to her, or whether she is the victim of bullying. Bullying will have the power imbalance that Sparrow talks about, it will have occurred repeatedly, and it will be obvious the perpetrator wants to hurt your daughter. If it amounts to bullying, it's important that girls know we are the adults, and we have this in hand, and we want to act on it, based on her information. Give her a voice in the decision. Confiscating her phone should not be the immediate response. Other things are important too, like collecting evidence including screenshots or messages. Then it's important to take action. That might include your daughter ignoring the bully, who just wants attention, or confiding in a teacher. You may make a complaint to the school or, in serious cases, contact police.

But what if the shoe is on the other foot and a parent learns that their child has been responsible for, or participated in, bullying? I asked every expert I could find that question, and the answers bore strong similarities. From the start, parents need to support each other, knowing their child is trying to navigate their way in the world. 'Accept the fact that our kids are going to screw up, and not take bad kids' behaviour as shaming to the parents,' one expert says. Of course, it's different if parents are ignoring their own child's repeated and bad behaviour, or even condoning it. But that's not the case with most parents, who are mortified to find their child is responsible for the unhappiness of another child. Be the person who drives your children to school and to sporting matches ... and listen in on the conversations – this was also a strong recommendation. In the back of the car, children will soon be lost in their own conversations. That provides a golden opportunity to learn how our child treats others and is treated in return. 'They'll start talking,' one expert says. 'You will hear the way they speak to each other. And you'll hear the way they speak about other kids, and that's going to give you a clue as to what your daughter is actually like.'

The shaming of children who bully rarely leads to victory. At ten, children are stretching the boundaries, struggling with self-esteem, learning to be funny – and sometimes that comes across as mean and sarcastic. But parents need to be aware of when it goes beyond that, recognise that their child needs assistance, and act. 'If it was my daughter,' one expert on tween girls explains, 'I would have no hesitation in going with her and having a couple of sessions with a child psychologist to unpack what's the appeal there and what would be a better way to respond.'

The nature of bullying – online and in person – is becoming more serious, younger. 'I know a girl who would whisper to a girl in the class, "You're pathetic – nobody wants you here,"' Sparrow says. In this case, the children were in Year 4. 'This is the stuff I would have once seen in Grade 9,' she says. This is offline bullying, and is common at the age of ten. But a tsunami of online texts – that range from little digs to demands that a girl take her life – is common in some friendship circles. Some children will not tell their parents. When asked why, they say that they're scared the bullies will find out and that it will make lunch hours even more unbearable.

But when they do confide in their parents, it's a difficult issue for adults to navigate. 'My twelve-year-old suffered terrible bullying in her last year of primary,' one mother told me. 'She lost her BFF to a mean girl and she still really struggles dealing with that and trying to understand why.' Her second friend joined the instigator. 'Then they made her life hell at school. They made everyone not talk to her; she would come home crying every day. She had weeks off because she just couldn't bear to go to school. It absolutely broke my heart.' Other parents mirror those views. 'She's so eager to keep everyone happy that she has been allowing herself to be bullied just to keep friends rather than go play with other friends,' one mother says.

It's a difficult issue for schools, too. 'I hate that the generic response from schools now is that she needs to be more resilient, without ever questioning the behaviour of the girls who are really quite unpleasant to her,' says a mum. Cyberbullying rarely happens between 8.30 am and 3.30 pm Monday to Friday. While sometimes it involves students in the same class or school, often it involves students in different schools. Privacy issues arise. Furthermore, different schools have different rules about the use of mobile phones and how bullying complaints are investigated. Parents sometimes stymie investigations, too. In one case, two fathers decided to sort it out in a hotel car park. But despite differences in protocols for handling it, one fact remains clear: it continues to happen to our children, and at an increasingly younger age.

While the plethora of devices on offer means a child might still be cyberbullied – or cyberbully others – non-ownership of a phone reduces the chances. Those who have a child who has been bullied or has been accused of bullying will tell you that the daily pestering for a smartphone is a more tolerable option than dealing with online mistakes. Dr Goodwin says most cyberbullying occurs at night, so for those children who do have phones, forbidding devices in bedrooms, and close to bedtime, can reduce the chance of bullying incidents arising. And a word of advice: parents of ten-year-olds should implement these strategies *now*. 'Going in and trying to remove a device from a fourteen-year-old or sixteen-year-old is near impossible,' Dr Goodwin says. Her advice is in agreement with that of others. Parents have to work together, find other mums and dads with similar approaches, and foster and forge friendships.

But what makes a ten-year-old girl, who has not shown any real unkindness to anyone previously, resort to bullying her peers? 'I think it's the perceived sense of anonymity,' Dr Goodwin says. 'They can test the boundaries but think in a way that they are unlikely to get caught. I actually think a big part of it's driven by that lack of impulse control.' 'Lack of impulse control' is crucial. As ten-year-olds, we all made impulsive decisions: spending all our pocket money on a silly purchase, or stopping off at a friend's on the way home from school without alerting our parents. But the consequences forty years ago were very, very different. 'I think we're replicating that but in a digital format,' Dr Goodwin says. The problem there is that each online 'mistake' leaves a clear digital DNA. 'And they often think that their digital DNA disappears. It's one snap on Snapchat, or one video that disappears, or one message and I can press delete. Or I can hide it.'

Explaining a digital footprint to a sixteen-year-old is mightily difficult; to a ten-year-old it's nigh on impossible. 'This is tricky,' Dr Goodwin says, 'because it's not on their radar, and I often say to parents – even when their children are sixteen – "I hate to tell you, but your sixteen-year-old daughter is not thinking about her career prospects."' When advising parents, Dr Goodwin suggests they tie the digital footprint concept to immediate consequences. One option is to talk about how being unkind to a friend might remove the opportunity to be soccer captain. Appealing to a young person's desire to lead is clever. In writing *Being 14*, I searched for those qualities a girl possessed that meant she ended up a school leader. Many were articulate, but not all. Many were bright, but some struggled at school. Most were gregarious, but some were certainly not. Principals pointed out that, almost always, a girl who ends up wearing a leader's badge is one who has been kind to others, who hasn't excluded peers and who doesn't see friendship as something to give and take back.

Sasha has been a Kids' Helpline counsellor for almost twenty years, and it's easy to imagine her warm voice giving comfort in some of the 4091 calls ten-year-olds made in the two years to December 2019. That's right, 4091 is how many times ten-year-old Australians dialled 1800 55 1800. Almost 2800 of those calls were for counselling on a specific issue, with family relationships, emotional wellbeing, bullying, friend relationships and child abuse being the top five counselling concerns. More than 70 per cent of those calls were from ten-year-old girls. Girls were much more likely than boys to be concerned about peer relationships (19 per cent versus 7 per cent), and for both boys and girls, bullying was the subject of 18 per cent of all contacts.[4]

These figures are an indictment on all of us. That many hundreds of children reached the point, with bullying, that they sought the advice of an independent counselling service is an indication of just how hard it is for our ten-year-olds to turn to the people closest to them for help. 'My teacher wouldn't understand,' they say. Or, 'Telling the teacher will make it worse', or 'Mum and Dad say to get over it', or 'Mum says to find new friends'. For a ten-year-old trapped in a world of hate, it can be all-consuming. Sasha remembers from the early days of her stint at Kids' Helpline that the advice being sought was straightforward. Many children were simply annoyed at Mum or Dad. But now, issues are more complex and grave, with a greater prevalence of mental health issues. Sasha says that some children will want to talk about the 'people being mean' to her; others are trying to map out what is happening, and some will ask for strategies to deal with it. 'I sometimes say, "Look, I'm really keen to understand this, and I'm actually writing down in my notebook about your group and that other group ..."' She'll ask for first names and what each of the players is like, and the conversation soon becomes an engrossing tale of friendship gone wrong, or friendship theft, or other issues around their friendship world. Often, they'll want her to take sides; their world will be black and white.

Sometimes a school guidance officer might refer a child, the victim of bullying, to Kids' Helpline to look at strategies to deal with the treatment being meted out to her. Sasha says incidences of 'really overt, targeted and patterned bullying' are few. On most occasions, the call will be more about misunderstandings, or friendship dramas. 'I'll say, "When you say they're mean to you and they won't play with you, what do you say before you go up to them?"' On more than one occasion, the child will have asked a group of friends to play imaginary ponies, but that group is not interested because they want to play handball.

This is why the age of ten can be so tricky. Some girls want to play make-believe games, others are beginning to be interested in boys. But they sit in the same class, and sometimes the same friendship circle. Drawn together by similar interests, they can soon be torn apart by the lack of commonality and their inability to deal with those differences. Sasha's focus is on listening. 'A distressed little ten-year-old just might need a gentle, comforting adult on the phone to listen. And just really, really listen,' she says. That's the job of parents, and perhaps it is one we can be better at, too, because the level of nastiness in some circles is beyond what we, at the same age, could have imagined. Susan McLean gives us examples . . . Girls, aged ten, ghosting peers. Girls, a bit older, taking turns to send a birthday invite to a particular girl, who turns up at an address where no-one else is. Girls working with others to shut out those they don't want to belong. 'I've seen children in primary school telling others to kill themselves,' McLean says. 'The level of nastiness can be terrible.' And those examples of nastiness all equal bullying.

Some schools do a stellar job here. Others don't, and the focus on empathy and kindness is often hidden behind the appeal of Maths and Science and History. Schools need to have clear procedures around dealing with complaints. They need a transparent and enforceable mobile phone policy. They need to ensure academic learning doesn't obscure those critical-thinking and so-called 'soft skills' that will determine whether our children succeed in whatever sphere they enter. As a community we need to do more too, like implementing 'right to erasure' laws and demanding stronger crackdowns on politicians and public figures who wage bullying campaigns against others.

But at the centre of any solution sit parents, who need to consider both when their child is given a smartphone and the parameters around its use, including the legal requirements. Every expert interviewed during this research encouraged parents to work with others who share similar views. We do that in infants' and primary school, stopping to chat at drop-off over everything from vaccinations to lunch boxes. It can't afford to stop when our girls reach those magic double-figures; we just need to find other ways of doing it. If our children are already on social media, parents need to know how to use it, have access to their child's password and regularly check their phone. They also need to ensure that any social media account is set to the highest privacy setting. Other measures are to ensure a child doesn't use a photo of herself or her real name, and to encourage a policy of not accepting friend requests from people she wouldn't greet at the local supermarket. Parental controls and apps need to be understood, and used.

Susan McLean has seen enough heartbreak amongst ten-year-olds to demand we do things differently. 'Parents should be the gatekeepers to their child's online world and their child's online safety,' she says. 'And if you don't do it, you're going to have problems. It's as simple as that.' And even if you do, you still might have problems. 'Good kids make poor choices,' McLean says, 'and especially during COVID, because kids wanted to connect. They wanted to be liked. They wanted to play the numbers game, and it's all just false.'

The take-out from experts here is clear: ten-year-olds need to value kindness and stand up for what is right, but they need to be taught those skills. During hearings of Queensland's Anti-Cyberbullying Taskforce, I met hundreds and hundreds of children, and received even more correspondence from parents. One niggling fact chases me to bed on some nights, and is still top of mind on many mornings. More children, at the age of ten and eleven and twelve, and even older, will ignore a peer being bullied rather than defend them. Why? Because they fear the bullies will turn on them. 'Snitches get stitches' was a term I hadn't heard for decades, until listening to these young students explain why they didn't pull up a peer bully. That reasoning is understandable, but it needs to change so that playgrounds and classes are filled with up-standers, not bystanders. As one expert put it, our children need the confidence to stand up for what is right, and the kindness to know when something is wrong. They need to know the lifelong value of friendship, and how to deal with it when things go wrong.

6

Confidence and self-esteem

'If I could teach them one thing, it would be:
stop comparing yourself. Don't do it . . . You
are enough. That's what you've got to know.'

Catherine O'Kane, principal, All Hallows' School

Paulina Skerman, Principal of Sydney's Santa Sabina College, is doing pre-enrolment interviews with nine-year-olds. She wants to know her students and what makes them tick, and she has a few standard questions to help her in this endeavour. One of these is to ask the girls to describe themselves in three words. 'I would say six times out of ten, maybe seven times out of ten, they would say "smart and kind",' Skerman says. She applauds this self-confidence. Janeen Fricke, principal of Mount Isa School of the Air, has the same experience. 'Sometimes, with ten-year-olds, we take them on camp and I've never seen kids more confident to get up and entertain. They will get up and sing and dance in front of anybody.'

'I am sweet, kind, funny, a good listener, creative and energetic,' one ten-year-old told me. And that delightful self-analysis was mirrored by most of the 500 others canvassed. Across Australia, from rural and remote communities like Mount Isa to big cities like Melbourne and Sydney, girls' answers were positive. And this was the case irrespective of whether they attended public schools, private schools, co-educational facilities or all-girls' colleges. Nine times out of ten, when asked directly to describe themselves, the answers were propitious – and playful.

'I am a crazy cat lady.'

'Funny, kind and I never give up.'

'I like helping people in all types of ways, especially if it involves food and cooking.'

'I think I am playful and musical.'

'I love chocolate and I'm kind and a bit funny.'

'I am amazing, nice, kind, funny, awesome and my gift is being annoying.'

'I love animals.'

'I am a funny girl who sometimes gets emotional. I LOVE cooking and I want to be famous.'

'I'm creative, a tomboy and pretty.'

It's hard to countenance those answers when we hear what they have to say only a year or so later; it's just one of the many emerging contradictions educators, professionals and parents see within this age group. For, sometime around or after ten, in too many cases that confidence and belief in themselves begins to falter. For many it unravels slowly, like a winter's night. For others it's with the speed of a friendship bust-up. One moment they will stand up in class in front of their peers and give their opinion, or hog the karaoke microphone at a family barbecue, and then the next week they won't. One week they will show that funny and playful side to everyone who will listen, and the next week they will stay quiet, waiting for someone else to take their place on centre-stage. Self-confidence is so important at ten, as girls begin to make decisions independently – about others and about themselves. This is the time, experts say, when they need to be able to draw on that childhood confidence, and in an unsporting irony it is also often the time when it suddenly wavers. So what happens that undermines the self-esteem of our girls and mutes that delightful self-confidence Paulina Skerman hears at pre-enrolment interviews?

Janeen Fricke in Mount Isa says the sphere of influence changes: away from family and other trusting adults, to peers. 'I think once they get to that age group, the audience is often their peers, and probably their peers shoot them down a bit more than what an adult crew would,' she says. More than 2330 kilometres away, in a different state and a different school setting, Paulina Skerman mirrors that view. 'I think they pull back and they start to compare themselves a little bit more with the outside world.' Hugh van Cuylenburg, author of *The Resilience Project*, says the judgement of others can be vicious. 'Early on we don't feel the judgement of others on us. We don't judge five-year-olds for singing and dancing at a party but then we do judge someone a little bit older. We start to look at them a little bit differently,' he says. At the age of ten, and eleven and twelve, self-consciousness sets in and it's about 'not wanting to stand out too much'. 'You don't want to be seen too much because you're already a bit insecure about the changes taking place,' he says.

This is the time when our girls hear what their peers say and take it as a verdict. They see how those in their class act. They listen to the messages delivered on television. They hear the words of songs they previously simply sang out loud to. And they see others like them, on social media feeds – who are really nothing like them – and feel demoralised. The comparison rarely lifts them, and the judgement they then make of themselves is often brutal.

This is something most parents spot quickly. One daughter, on the trip home from school, asked her mother why they didn't live in a house like her new BFF. She was embarrassed, she told her mother. Those comparisons – on parental jobs, style of home and how the family spends its leisure time – were common. But more concerning, perhaps, was the verdict girls delivered on themselves. 'I'm just not very interesting,' one ten-year-old says. Or, 'I'm too shy to join in.' Parents are concerned. 'I wish she knew her worth and knows that she is loved for who she is and doesn't need to be perfect,' one mother says. Another says, 'My main concern is probably her self-criticism and when she says negative things about herself or worries too much about the opinions of others.' And a third: 'She cares too much about what others think and changes who she is to fit in and be liked.' And so it goes on.

> 'I just want her to be confident with who she is and love herself as she is.'

> 'She is amazing but she doesn't see it.'

> 'She needs to believe in herself more. She gives her friends all this amazing advice and doesn't take it herself.'

> 'I want her to understand that the most important person to accept her is herself.'

'I worry that she wants to crush the qualities that are great because others her age don't think they are.'

Many teachers, inside classrooms, science labs and out on the sporting field, nominate dwindling confidence levels as the significant challenge they see facing ten-year-old girls. They see this self-judgement raise its head in class teamwork, in their shrinking passion to try out for sport, in who they choose as friends, and in their frenzied attempts to fit in. They see them lose a little bit of themselves in order to be a little bit more like someone else. 'I wish they could find their own identity among their peers,' one Year 5 teacher says. And while friendship and social media and body image are repeatedly raised as key challenges by teachers of ten-year-olds, 'self-esteem' and 'self-confidence' are constant themes.

Here are some answers teachers gave to the question, 'What do you see as the biggest challenge facing the ten-year-olds you teach?'

'Self-confidence.'

'Confidence in self.'

'Self-esteem and identity.'

'How they see themselves.'

'Identity and self-worth. Acceptance of self.'

'Self-worth from within; not having to be validated by others either online or face to face.'

And what do teachers believe is the reason why their students' self-belief can so quickly fall off a cliff? Managing expectations of parents and peers; navigating an online world where feeds are brimming with what they believe they are not; and a newfound determination to look outside their families, outside themselves, at how others see them.

Enter the 'looking-glass self', a theory developed by American sociologist Charles Horton Cooley and published in 1902. The concept is terrific for understanding how a girl's developing identity can be distorted. It works like this: we see our reflection as we think it appears to others. So a girl decides what she thinks of herself by deciding what others think of her. 'It's not necessarily what people are thinking of them but what they imagine people might be thinking of them,' says Karen Young, founder of website *Hey Sigmund*. She says it's at the age of about ten that adolescents start the job of determining who they want to be. Until then, it was largely done for them. 'They look up and go, "Well, who do I want to be? Who are the adults I want to be in the world? What do I want myself to look like as I grow up?"' Their whole self-concept gets a mighty work-out. 'Now it's a healthy thing that their self-concept gets a work-out because we want them to start thinking about who they want to be,' Young says. 'But that self-concept during adolescence is often based on what they think other people think of them – the looking-glass self.

This is a time when parents might see their ten-year-olds starting to pull away from them. That's part of the journey to self-identity. This doesn't mean that girls don't need us; they absolutely do. But their peers become a new and important source of information and navigation. 'They have access to so much information,' Young says. 'And a lot of that is through social media, but they're also looking around and they're comparing themselves around the marks they get, how they look in comparison to other kids, what they have, what they are wearing and what they don't have.' Overwhelmingly, experts spoke against the standardised testing we see in our classrooms. Psychologists, school counsellors and educators warned that it could flatten the curiosity, self-esteem and even potential of our girls. In terms of self-confidence, some say, increased testing has become almost as insidious as social media. It leads many girls to believe 'I'm not smart enough' or 'I'm not good enough' or 'I might be really good at English, but I'm not good at Maths so I'm stupid'.

Having no access to social media is not a protection against the influence it wields. The messages are on their friends' feeds, on the pop-up ads on their computer, on television, on billboards and in shop windows. They see it wherever they look, and from these sources the question 'What should I look like?' is answered in a very narrow way. 'They use that information as the ideal,' Young says. 'And if [they're] short of the ideal, they think they don't measure up. That's what they are imagining, and that's when I think it can start to cause problems.' Those problems run the gamut: some girls withdraw, some become less confident, some see themselves in unflattering ways. It can dent their self-esteem, determine how they want to be seen, and create anxiety and other mental health challenges. Self-harm, which I discuss elsewhere, is increasing amongst girls and is starting at a younger age. 'What I'm getting from those conversations are: "I'm not pretty." "I'm not smart."' Young says. 'And sometimes it's kind of nebulous: "I'm just not good enough." They can't really articulate what it is, but it's a sense of just not being enough, and that is happening really young, and that's bothering me.'

Helen Adams, head of junior school at St Mary's Anglican Girls' School in Perth, says she sees peer pressure as a big player in diminishing self-confidence levels. 'That's when they want to be wearing the same as someone else; self-doubt comes in.' Schoolwork also becomes more complex at this stage, with children being required to work more independently than previously. 'Peer pressure, the complexity of the work, senior school looming ... these things concern them. Their bodies are also changing and they're feeling a little bit physically awkward.'

While some experts believe a supportive family that encourages independent decision-making can boost self-confidence, there's not necessarily 'rhyme nor reason' in every case. 'Sometimes you look at the parents and they're super-confident and the girls aren't,' Helen Adams says. And in other cases, it's the opposite. That doesn't mean a parent's role in fostering self-confidence is not important; it is crucial, and every expert suggests starting it as early as we can so those foundations are built slowly and solidly. Then, by the time girls reach adolescence and begin the job of experimenting with their independence, they've got a convincing self-view and a belief that they are strong. 'They need to know what strong looks like, what brave looks like, what beautiful looks like. We can put those ideas onto them,' Karen Young says. Understanding their need for independence is also crucial. When they are five and six and seven, we buy into every decision, and often make it for them. As they grow we question the decisions they make. How that's done is important. If their take-out of our questioning is shame, or a feeling that they are unable to make good decisions, or even that their opinion is wrong, they will look elsewhere for validation. Language, again, is crucial.

I explored a father's role in positive engagement in my last book, *Fathers and Daughters*. One of the overpowering messages I got from my research was that we need to encourage our daughters' developing opinions, even if we disagree with them. (After all, we never agreed with everything our own parents said or did ...) Just as a father can build a daughter's self-esteem, he can also crush it quickly. If, for example, he demolishes an argument posed by his daughter without properly hearing it or considering it, then the subtext he delivers is this: you are not smart; you don't get it; you are immature. Our daughters see this as a 'put-down', and the hit to their self-esteem can drive a sharp wedge between father and daughter. These are typical reactions of girls I spoke to during that research:

> *'Dad just says I'm wrong when I try to say what I think – so I don't bother anymore.'*

> *'I just go quiet. I try and say something – like on refugees – and he just slaps my argument down.'*

> *'Why bother? I'm not allowed to have an independent view. And I'm not about to agree with Dad and his views on same-sex marriage.'*

One senior educator says that fathers need to leave being QC in the courtroom, or business manager at the office, and remember they are only ever Dad at home. Others quickly pointed out an irony in how some fathers – and mothers – treat their teen daughters' opinions. Our girls are being schooled to have convictions, to analyse the different sides of an argument, to find the supporting evidence and then to prosecute it with passion and clarity. Parents support this in the school context. The resurgence in the popularity of public speaking and debating is evidence of that. But then the girls come home and, in many cases, their parents will object to them having an independent view.

Experts say parents should be proud of their daughter's attempts to show off her knowledge or test out a theory. And we need to put aside any opposition and look for the intellectual engagement our daughters are offering. That journey to finding their voice is crucial. Melbourne psychologist and author Andrew Fuller does an exercise with girls of this age. He gets them to pair up and then asks them to say 'no' until their partner is convinced they really mean 'no'. He then gets them to swap positions and do the same. 'It's the first time that many of those girls have ever emphatically said "no" to anyone,' he says. 'At some stage in your life, particularly [for] young women, a guy's going to try it on and you need to able to say, "No, that's not what I want. I'm not interested." And if you've never done it – if you've never actually said those words, emphatically – how can you do it? You can't do it.' Fuller sees the consequences of acquiescence with girls a few years older. Some of them might come to his consulting room having had sex the night before. They tell him, 'I didn't really want it but I went along with it because I didn't know what else to do.' Finding one's voice is important to be able to say 'yes', but just as important to be able to say 'no'. It is 'powerfully embracing', Fuller says, to know what you want and to be able to reject what you don't.

Many principals nominate self-esteem and confidence as the key ingredients for girls succeeding, and curricula have been scoped out in many schools to help increase girls' confidence and to allow them to see themselves as leaders. This is particularly a focus in all-girls schools, with an array of leadership positions spanning academic, sporting and social pursuits. Girls are taught you don't need a badge to be a leader, and encouraged to take 'active leadership' in everything from school gardening projects to charity drives.

Confident children show it in their body language, says Kym Amor, principal of Foxwell State Secondary College in Coomera, on the northern tip of Queensland's Gold Coast. 'You can look out and physically see it . . . in the body language and non-verbals.' She gives the example of a child walking through the school gates and joining a group of girls for a chat. 'They'll walk up and say good morning to any children who are there, and [have] the social skills to create connections, regardless of their friendship group.' Helen Adams says she's learnt to pick those with strong self-confidence, too. Often they became natural leaders. 'And you see that from quite a young age. It's not the alpha female, but they're strong; they still have that very strong self-belief,' she says. While school principal Toni Riordan acknowledges that some ten-year-olds have no problems with self-esteem, she maintains that for those who do, it can be nurtured and grown. It can also be modelled, and older students are encouraged to do that.

Brisbane school psychologist Tara McLachlan says self-compassion is the antidote to low self-esteem. Girls can be so hard on themselves, she explains. She has spent many hours encouraging them to be kind and compassionate to themselves, as well as to others. 'It's not just having a bubble bath or putting a face mask on. It's about the way that you talk to yourself,' she says. Girls need to be encouraged to check on themselves and consider whether they are being overly negative or critical. They need to learn to stop and say, 'That's not a very nice way to talk to myself', and shift to a kinder stance – like they would talk to a best friend or someone they love dearly. I love this, because it also encourages a different way of seeing the looking-glass self: to look in the mirror and see whether they would be as hard on a friend as they are on themselves. 'It's being able to choose the kindest route rather than just keep pushing themselves to do more and more,' McLachlan says. She makes the point that research has shown interventions are not necessarily always effective in shifting damaged or low self-esteem. Self-compassion is a different approach. It fosters thought and care. 'I think, in primary school, if they could start doing some work on self-care and self-compassion, that would be so important,' she says. 'These girls just work so hard. They have all their co-curricular activities, they prioritise their friends, and girls in particular I think put everyone else first. They'll put a friend before themselves. It's important, McLachlan says, that girls 'shift the focus to what's best for them – filling up their cups so that they can then be a better friend and daughter'.

In their widely acclaimed book, *The Confidence Code for Girls*, authors Katty Kay and Claire Shipman tell girls to imagine confidence as a 'tiny, powerful coach inside your mind helping you do all the things you want to do'.[1] Given a wand, and one magic spell, that's exactly what principal Kym Amor would bring to every ten-year-old girl. 'My magical power for ten-year-old girls is a personal superpower that allows them to retain their inner beauty and innocence, vulnerability and hope, whilst able to provide a force field of strength, courage, determination, grit and resilience that will allow them to know their self-worth, stand true to their beliefs, and always aspire to fulfil their *own* aspirations,' she says.

7

Resilience and grit

'We need to teach our girls to know how to actively
lobby for what they need and deserve, how to
speak up in a culture that often tries to silence
them, and how to be clear and unapologetic
when expressing their own personal boundaries.'

Dannielle Miller, founder, Enlighten Education

Hugh van Cuylenburg reckons Stanzin, a nine-year-old
child he met at a mudbrick school in an Indian village
2400 kilometres from Mumbai, is the kindest person alive.
Van Cuylenburg met Stanzin when he went to teach at
the little school set on the Himalayan desert plain. On his
first day he walked into a classroom and, not realising
how low the doorframe was set, smacked his head on
the lintel. 'I reeled about, clutching my head like I was
Kramer in an episode of *Seinfeld*,' he later wrote in his

book *The Resilience Project*. 'I had never seen a group of kids laugh so much in my entire life.'[1] The next day, van Cuylenburg arrived at the classroom to be greeted by a smiling Stanzin. Van Cuylenburg looked up at the doorframe to see that sand and leaves had been skilfully wrapped in cloth and tied to the spot where he had previously whacked his head. Stanzin had done the same thing to every door, in an effort to protect his new teacher.

It wasn't just that episode that showed off the child's precocious kindness. At lunchtime, in the rudimentary playground, Stanzin constantly checked in with his classmates. On one occasion he forfeited a cricket game to play with a female friend he spotted sitting by herself. Outside of class, he visited those who were sick and unable to make it to school.

One evening, heading home to his lodgings after a day of teaching, van Cuylenburg spotted Stanzin, in his school uniform, bedding down on the street. His face wore a smile that stretched from ear to ear. Hugh van Cuylenburg says he fought the urge to burst out crying. 'I didn't sleep a wink that night,' he recalls. 'I thought of all the people I knew back in Australia and the students I'd taught over the years who'd struggled with depression, anxiety and other mental illnesses. Why were we in the developed world so broken? Why were we in Australia, such a beautiful and privileged country, so anxious and depressed?'

The student Stanzin soon turned teacher, and each day Hugh van Cuylenburg would find himself studying this happy-go-lucky young man, and other locals, whose kindness radiated across the village. He took notes, asked questions and tried to understand what lay behind the natural happiness of the locals. And it led him, back in Australia, to focus on teaching our own children three principles he believes provide a foundation for resilience: gratitude, empathy and mindfulness. Forced to pick the most valuable of the three, he says it would be mindfulness. 'That's because I think it allows the other two to flourish really naturally. So if you're someone who is very good at being where you are, at being present, you will notice the things around you. You also notice opportunities to be there for other people.' The resonance is in that last sentence: being there for other people. Indeed, many experts believe that resilience is built more from *doing* rather than *feeling*; it is about being competent and service-oriented.

Andrew Fuller, a hugely popular author and a rock star in the world of teen psychologists, disputes that resilience is a big issue amongst ten-year-old girls. He says his research of 193 000 young people shows that 'the social turbulence of Years 3 to 4 has passed and transition is yet to occur'. He says, 'Students are overwhelmingly positive and engaged, and we need to capitalise on that momentum.'

But perception can sometimes be as difficult to deal with as reality. These answers from parents – particularly mothers – as to what their number one concern is for their tween girl, are revealing.

'She needs a growth mindset and to realise that everything won't always be easy for her.'

'She used to dance to the beat of her own drum but I worry that's disappearing with the desire to conform.'

'I want her to know she has a voice and her opinion is valued, something I struggled with as a child and still to some extent as an adult.'

The 'R word' is raised again and again:

'Resilience. To take a deep breath when things go wrong and shake it off.'

'She is a high achiever in most areas and hasn't really experienced much disappointment. I wonder how she will cope when things don't turn out well.'

'She cries a lot over nothing. It could be her siblings, or having to walk too far. I wish she would toughen up.'

'Lack of resilience and self-belief. She is way more awesome and amazing and smart than she seems to believe or give herself credit for.'

'I'd love her to be more willing to try new things and to tough out things she finds hard. She quits too soon.'

'She can start crying over the smallest thing.'

I'll come to self-regulation shortly, but Andrew Fuller believes many of these children might present differently at home than they do at school. 'Basically, Grade 5 and Grade 6 is a time of incredible capacity. They are quite resilient,' he says. 'At home with their parents might be different to what they truly are. I think it's easy to under-estimate kids a bit,' he says.

So what do their teachers think? Some common themes emerged when teachers were asked about how they perceive resilience amongst their ten-year-old charges.

'Varies greatly. Those with outside interests show more resilience.'

'Limited; they're fragile and preoccupied with their distractions. Those with higher resilience come from families with structure, routine and strict protocols, and a culture of reading/adventure.'

'I think the level of resilience really depends on the experiences they've had. Some have high levels of resilience and will usually be confident in themselves, but also still [be] quiet – they are not the loud, "out-there" girls. Some will easily cry and show little resilience over small

issues – they usually also show signs of anxiety or are the loud, out-there girls trying to mask their insecurities.'

'It is very varied – I think there is a strong link between parental expectations and if a student has perfectionistic traits. The students with higher resilience tend to be more comfortable with their own view of themselves, are more willing to try new things, are active listeners and readily give encouragement to others. They also are usually more self-sufficient and don't require others so much for validation.'

'Higher-resilience students tend to be more confident in themselves, whereas low-resilience students need feedback and validation constantly.'

The role parents play in engendering resilience is apparent. Here is the assessment of four teachers:

'There are common traits in kids with higher resilience, like strong parental support in their early years and open family discussions with clear, positive behaviour expectations.'

'I have noticed the students who are more resilient come from families who have parents who are easygoing and resilient themselves. However, I find students who are not very resilient seem to come from families who worry, are over-protective and lack problem-solving skills.'

'Those who are more resilient usually come from homes where parents don't bubble-wrap their children every step of the way.'

'Parents who allow their children to "fail", not rescue or problem-solve for them but cheerlead from the sideline ... [this] definitely makes a difference in how a ten-year-old responds to challenging situations.'

Those who had faced adversity, like illness, early in their lives were also mentioned by teachers as having more resilience. Andrew Fuller, whose own daughter survived childhood leukaemia, says this is a common belief in cancer wards. 'Kids with cancer are sometimes tearaway teenagers, willing to do anything. They have both: a derring-do and a fragility.' Another view that emerged was that rural children were generally more resilient. This observation was supported by boarding school educators and those who had worked in both rural and metropolitan areas. Janeen Fricke, principal of the Mount Isa School of the Air, says, 'One of the things that we do notice is that our children are really resilient.' They see big worldly problems, not the tiny ones. They're watching their parents struggle with drought, on isolated stations, and understand a bigger picture perhaps than ten-year-olds in the warm embrace of a city: 'It might be weather-induced problems, or an accident, or the life cycle of animals living and dying, but they're really in touch with that side of life.' Fricke makes a link between this and their ability to both solve problems and use networks. 'So if you're in an isolated station, and there's a problem, your next-door neighbour is probably going to help, or the Royal Flying Doctor Service, or people on the side of the road. You all pull together. They know they have to problem-solve to deal with difficult situations, and that tomorrow still exists. I think there's a real resilience in a community sense.'

What's interesting is when country children move to the city to attend boarding school, or to stay with cousins and attend day school. Fricke says she increasingly has to 'do a lot of work around' body image and anxiety in preparation for the move to the city. 'Whether it's after Year 6 or Year 10, it's then they get exposed to human behaviours that they've never had to deal with. And that's where they don't have resilience because they're not used to people not working together.' So can we learn something from our country cousins? 'Probably backing each other. Particularly when stress hits, you have got to have others around you who can help you.'

Helen Adams, a Perth junior school educator, says those with resilience have been allowed to 'bumble along without Mum mollycoddling them'. Another educator says, 'Some mums won't let them fail. And those are the girls who, when things go a little bit pear-shaped, do not cope. Whereas the ones who almost drag themselves up, to a certain degree, seem to be stronger, seem to roll a little bit more with those punches when things don't go according to plan.'

So what does resilience look like in a ten-year-old? Andrew Fuller says his experience is that ten-year-olds now are smarter than the previous generation, and many are good problem-solvers. 'In terms of creative and critical thinking, they're very good. Where they struggle often is in disruption in friendships, how to repair a relationship, and often [they] may become overly concerned about minor setbacks in their life so they freak out.' Any of us can 'freak out' when we are challenged, but it's how we deal with it that matters. 'For some people,' continues Fuller, 'you can then become avoidant to the situation and go, "Well, I'll never do that again because basically it was just too hard." But for others there will be a kind of over-focus on achieving in that area that can also be a form of not being resilient.' The one hundred teachers whose advice I sought nominated similar characteristics when it came to identifying those who showcased resilience in their classrooms. These were: the ability to work independently; not having the same driving need to fit in as some of their peers; a better self-concept; more positivity; better problem-solving skills; the ability to bounce back from disagreements; and fewer tears.

Tears. That word pops up repeatedly with parents and teachers – and it raises the issue of self-regulation, which Fuller says research shows is one of the strongest predictors of success. This includes developing executive functions like will-power, decision-making, planning abilities and emotional regulation. 'So when I'm feeling grumpy and anxious and tetchy, how do I learn to deal with that? And when I'm feeling flat and uninterested and bored and avoidant, how do I learn to deal with that?' Self-regulation is also a research focus of Associate Professor Kate Williams from the Queensland University of Technology. She says about 30 per cent of young children have difficulty here, and it can be seen across three areas: emotional regulation, attentional regulation and impulse control. With a ten-year-old, emotional regulation might be influenced by temperament but it might also be affected by being tired or by hormones playing havoc with her young body. Attentional regulation – the second area – relates to her ability to focus or persist with tasks, while the third, impulse control, relates largely to executive function – how our daughters are able to stop themselves making impulsive decisions. Crucially, all these work together.

The tie between self-regulation and wellbeing is also critical, says Williams. 'We have been able to link, in our studies, early self-regulation – even as young as four or five and absolutely it would still be predictive at ten – [to] things like adult mental health and psychological distress, gambling, substance abuse, teen substance abuse, self-harm,' she says. 'So if you can build those self-regulation skills early, you will drop the risk of those things happening drastically.'

But while self-regulation may be a necessary component of resilience, it is probably not sufficient on its own. Says Williams, 'I think of resilience as a longer-term thing, where you need to experience some adversities and then you need to come out the other side still okay. And that takes time.' While resilience and self-regulation come from different schools of thought, parents could improve the self-regulation of their daughter's emotions. Indeed, many parents sought advice on this matter. By the age of ten, says Williams, 'they're clever little cookies': 'They've got a lot of thinking skills that they can use, and you can start to talk to them about strategies that they're using for emotional regulation. There are two strategies we talk about in the research. One is called suppression, and that's where you just bury those feelings deep down inside and move on. And that's generally considered not a great approach in most circumstances.' The second one, cognitive reappraisal, is where a situation is considered in a different way, which can then impact emotions in a different way. 'So with ten-year-old girls, you can do something that you can't do with toddlers, which is talk about how the way we think about things affects how we feel about things ... If we change our thinking about it, can we change our feeling about it?'

But how much should parents worry if their ten-year-old is still bursting out crying over trivial matters? According to Williams, it might depend on the location. If the outburst is at school, regularly, or at a friend's place, or in a shopping mall, it is more cause for concern than at home. 'If they're falling apart just at home, what that's telling you is that they do have self-regulation skills and just run out of puff by the time they get home, and you're going to love them anyway, so you have to weather the storm of the tears and the rage.' This mirrors Fuller's point about the likelihood that our daughters are more resilient when we, their parents, are not watching.

Music can also play a role in developing self-regulation, according to Williams, who is a registered music therapist. She cites this example: When her husband played his music of choice at home, her then-ten-year-old would complain it made her 'dizzy'. She'd say, 'That makes me feel yuck, can you turn it off?' She'd then put on her own boppy music and her mood would instantly change. 'So really, letting them use music as a tool, and talking to them about that, from about ten, is good.' That's because the older our daughters get, the more music becomes a part of their social lives and the more they need to understand how the music they listen to affects their moods. Hugh van Cuylenburg also sings the praises of music – along with exercise and laughter – to help us feel more positive. In primary school, those three activities take up a chunk of the day, both in the curriculum and in the playground. But at middle school structured music lessons begin to trail off for many girls, and that needs attention. 'A lot of kids are self-conscious at that stage, so getting involved in music is probably a little bit harder – but we definitely need to have more,' van Cuylenburg says.

All of this is tricky, and even the link between self-confidence, self-esteem and resilience is not linear. Andrew Fuller concurs. 'It is not a neat link,' he says. 'It's interesting because what we see is that some of our most optimistic, high-self-esteem kids can actually fall apart quite quickly. While intuitively you'd think that higher self-esteem is going to lead to higher resilience, it's not always true.' But principals often spot resilience at the age of ten. Many of them raised, unprompted, the notion that it lights up a path to leadership. Retired Adelaide principal Kevin Tutt says those showing self-confidence and showcasing resilience frequently become class or school leaders. At his school, primary education ends in Year 5 and the junior school has its own captains. 'The two girls there at the moment . . . you can see a maturity about them – but it's the right maturity with respect to really good values,' he says. That came, he says, from their families. 'The value side of parenting is increasingly important.'

Most parents define resilience as having the flexibility to ride the setbacks of life. Fuller agrees, and adds quickly that it is a learnable skill. 'You learn it partly by learning about yourself as a person – as a capable human being. So the person to really know is yourself – what your strengths are ... and how to use those. And then it's about learning about your social support network and how you call upon them,' he says. This, as we've seen, is exactly what Janeen Fricke sees in her rural students. Fuller continues, 'You learn it by doing it. You don't learn *about* it; you learn by *being* it.' Brisbane school principal Catherine O'Kane agrees. 'It's looking outside themselves,' she says, 'and then that feeds through to their ability to bounce back when things don't go their way.' She says it was interesting listening to the most recent group of Year 12 girls, who had their final year upended by COVID-19. Some struggled, while most considered themselves fortunate not to have been sick and to have been able to do school online. 'They're a lot older than ten, but it's the same thing,' she says.

Dannielle Miller is the founder of Enlighten Education, a program delivered through school workshops to help teenagers develop self-esteem and confidence. She sees 'service learning opportunities' as a key to developing both self-confidence and resilience. 'Often people will talk to me about wanting to build more confident kids,' she says. Many of those people believe that should be done through teaching them more assertive language and body language skills. 'I think confidence comes from competence,' says Miller, 'and true confidence doesn't come necessarily from how you stand or what language you use, it comes more from realising that you are a person of capacity and that you are a person who can contribute. And that's why service learning is so powerful, because it contributes to that, too.' Miller sees it in the projects that students take on under her guidance – like the school toilet project, where students drive renovations to improve their facilities. This is clever. Renovating – through a splash of bright paint, the odd piece of school artwork, good locks, clean hand towels, flowers, moisturiser and soap – can change the tone of the building and the mood of its students. It allows children to be change-makers and build skills, from problem-solving to networking to time management – all valuable for later life. A sausage sizzle, for charity, didn't provide the same skills. 'They really just want the sausage; that's the truth. Getting them to actively contribute to causes that they're passionate about, and interested in, is a really wonderful way of building up their resilience and their altruism,' Miller says.

8

Body image

'If they truly, deeply want to live a full and joyous
and adventurous life, being at home and being at
peace with their body is where it all begins. Your
body is not an ornament in life, it is a vehicle
to your dreams. It's a vehicle to your goals. It's
a vehicle for adventures. Your body is to be
enjoyed. Nourish it, respect it, love it, embrace it.'

Taryn Brumfitt, author and leader, Body Image Movement

Ava is shopping with her Mum. She's ten. Feisty.
Articulate. And unsure. Her mother wants to buy
her a new swimsuit. Ava wants to get one, just not the
two-piece that her mother has chosen. 'I feel like I have a
bit of a belly,' she explains. Her friends, who are listening
to the story a few days later, all nod. 'My parents say that
when I get older it's going to stretch out and be okay.

But I think I have a really big rib cage.' She stands up in front of her friends and holds her hands stiff against her side. 'See, you can see the outline.' She traces an invisible line down one side of her body. Her friends all nod in agreement. 'So even if I do like them, I don't want to wear them because my belly sticks out. They're also too revealing for someone who looks like me.'

Ava says she is witty, a good reader and great at sport, but her body? Well, she just lost out there. And it seems the six friends she is sitting with know exactly how she feels. 'My friend, she's really skinny,' says Samantha, who has just turned eleven, 'and sometimes when I have to play with her and then I go home, I feel like I need to lose weight very quickly. She makes me feel bad.' And so it goes around this small table of ten- and eleven-year-olds. Fat arms; a gap in her teeth; too fat for dance now; and tall. Tall seems especially bad. 'I don't fit in, especially since I'm quite tall,' Mia says. 'I usually kind of feel like an outsider.' Alexis says she is tall, too. 'I know, right. It just means you have no friends. I wish there was a way of not being tall.'

Being too tall is like being too 'fat'. Girls aged nine, ten and eleven raised their height as a flaw in their appearance repeatedly. It's a perception around which so much work has been done, and so much said, in academic papers and research across the globe. Yet the facts speak for themselves. Just take these figures: more than half of all girls (between 55 and 59 per cent) and about one-third of boys (33 to 35 per cent) aged six to eight believe their ideal bodies are thinner than their current body.[1] Nearly one-third of children aged five to six nominate an ideal body size that is thinner than the size they believe they are,[2] and most ten-year-olds are more afraid of becoming fat than they are of war, cancer or losing their parents.[3] 'My biggest worry is my weight,' says one girl. And the same words fall from the mouths of ten-year-old girls in cities and towns across Australia. School counsellor Marcelle Nader-Turner says she remembers sitting with friends at lunchtime, as sixteen-year-olds, not eating but talking about how hungry they were. Now that is happening at half that age. Body image issues also rate in the Mission Australia National Youth Survey as one of the top concerns each year. That has led to a lobby to make body image a national mental health concern.[4]

So what is body image? What causes a negative body image? More importantly, what can we do to help Ava and Samantha and Mia and Alexis and every other young girl struggling with this? If we roll all definitions into one, the term 'body image' essentially means how we see and feel and behave towards our body. A healthy body image exists when we feel good about our body, an unhealthy body image when we think about our body in a negative or bleak way. In short, it's our perspective on our body and how we look. That's on paper. But when you see it around a table of ten-year-olds, or in notes they write about their body, or when you question them about what they like about themselves, body image takes on a much more sinister definition. It's something that gets under the skin of our daughters, that determines what they eat and what they wear, how they interact with their friends, and even whether they continue to don a sporting uniform and join a team. 'I worry about how other people feel about me,' one girl says. 'I always try to fit in by being myself but it doesn't work all the time. I am self-conscious about my body and height.' 'I worry that I will be an average-height girl,' says another. 'I worry about being overweight,' says another again. And all those answers were in response to this question: 'What do you worry about most?'

Causes of unhealthy body images are varied, but the ties to self-esteem, depression and eating disorders are undeniable. So is the fact that it can be a learned behaviour. Susan Dalton, principal of Miami State High School, would gladly make it disappear. 'It's okay to be the shape you are,' she says. 'You're ten!' You can hear the exasperation in her voice. School psychologist Tara McLachlan says body image issues can be heartbreaking, because girls often want to change what is not possible. 'It's so hard when it's something like the colour of their skin, or their height, or things that they just can't change about themselves,' she says. 'And I think it starts at ten – they just want to fit in and be like everyone else. So if everyone else is taller, they just want to be the same. They want to fit in.'

For tweens, reminders of how they want to look are omnipresent. Body consciousness saturates what they hear, looms large on billboards and in smartphone ads and is the talk at lunchtime, in sports change rooms and at dance classes. Author Rebecca Sparrow observed it in her own niece. 'I saw this girl who never cared what anyone thought and had a go at things suddenly being so self-conscious, and then worrying about her own body . . . And it's the opposite of the household she's been raised in,' she says. 'We have to have . . . conversations about body shapes.' There's no doubt the best time for that is well before girls are even cognisant of their bodies. That's when their parents are still the loudest voice they hear. 'Using this time wisely, to connect with our kids and to be that wise person to help unpack things with them, is key – before they turn more and more to their friends.'

That timing question is crucial, because a distorted body perception often magnifies as a girl leaps towards her teens and into adulthood. A Queensland study showed that almost 40 per cent of girls aged fifteen to nineteen feel 'extremely concerned' or 'very concerned' about their body image, compared with only 12 per cent of teen boys.[5] This view colours what they eat, who they date, how many hours they spend at the gym and how often they wear make-up. Sydney principal Paulina Skerman conducts interviews with her young students. 'I have a little giggle when I say that we don't have make-up here at school, so when you get to Grade 11 and 12, you know, no false eyelashes!' The girls laugh and are shocked that false eyelashes could ever be 'a thing' at school. But they are in many, many schools. 'That's very much a part of a sixteen- to seventeen-year-old girl's world,' Skerman says. 'False eyelashes, and some may even be experimenting with a bit of Botox.' She is supported by other principals in making this point: everything we can do to slow down this race by girls to grow up, we should do.

How a girl views her body will be influenced by many factors, but mainly by her peers, technology and the role played by her family, particularly her mother. Let's start with peer influence – something Mount Isa School of the Air principal Janeen Fricke raises. Fashion is big in country areas, particularly around the campdraft scene, but body image kicks in, very often, when the girls go away to boarding school. 'This is just from listening to parents whose kids go off to boarding school,' says Fricke. 'There's often this change: "Mum, we don't want to wear that stuff anymore. We want to see what's at Forever New."' It's not just how they *look*, she adds, it also comes with increased pressure for the latest in everything, and particularly anything electronic, including smartphones and headphones. Other educators share this observation: the girls want to look like someone else – the girl sitting next to them in class, or the girl on that television show or that YouTube channel, or on the bus. It's a matter of wanting to be the same. 'I want to look like Katie,' one girl says. Why? 'She just looks awesome.' Pressed to describe her, it's about her hair, and the fact that 'she's just the right height' and she 'always looks good'. This girl is not any exception to any rule. Too often, our ten-agers simply believe they are not enough.

School counsellor Tara McLachlan says that girls' single focus on their friends is problematic. 'It's so hard for them not to judge themselves when they hear their friends judging themselves,' she says. Increasingly, schools are now talking to girls about what they eat: the importance of breakfast, and that it is how their body works, not how it looks, that matters. Breakfast, though, can be a prickly issue to navigate, because some girls who experience anxiety are not hungry early in the morning. Others wake up late and race out the door to make the bus on time. 'We talk to them about just trying to have something, like a piece of fruit or a smoothie – something like that. But having the three meals a day is really, really important,' McLachlan says. 'We encourage girls to eat in order to fuel their bodies and minds. We want to shift the focus from physical appearance, weight and shape to self-care, health and emotional wellbeing.'

The perception of how teens should look and feel is also fed by what they consume, in the form of media.

Statistics from the United States ram that home. The average body mass index (BMI) of Miss America winners decreased from around 22 in the 1920s to 16.9 in the 2000s. (A normal BMI falls between 18.5 and 24.9.)[5] In a world where Instagram influencers can make a tidy income from doing nothing but looking thin and telling others how to do it, social media has a lot to answer for. At ten, girls' brains are still developing, and their ability to analyse the meaning of the messages they receive is far from complete. Cyber-safety expert Susan McLean says many girls will think the doctored photographs filling their screens are genuine. 'If they have access to social media, then they are getting this total news feed of images that you and I know are photoshopped. You and I know they aren't real,' she says. Girls need to be taught to analyse critically what they see and hear.

The coronavirus pandemic has brought with it some-thing scary, McLean says. She knows of numerous cases where teachers tried to provide lessons – academic and performing arts – via Zoom or a similar platform. Children as young as ten refused, because they were required to appear on video and didn't like the way they looked. 'I'm getting lot of parents concerned about how their kids are feeling,' she says. Author and girl advocate Dannielle Miller says body image as an issue has become increas-ingly complex over time. Photographs of 'perfect' bodies used to appear in the pages of magazines for women; now they are online. 'That means girls are being exposed to them at a younger age,' she says – and in greater quantities. When we were ten, we might have bought *Dolly* magazine, but not something for older women. Now girls are following celebrities that are across Instagram, not specific magazines. That brings with it lavish doses of both uncertainty and pressure. 'They are growing up in this landscape,' says Miller. 'And they'll be wondering where they will fit into that. "Is that what I am meant to look like? An adored, likeable, influential young woman? I don't look anything like that at the moment. How's that going to happen?"'

This is the age where girls also become more aware of branding. 'It's not enough just to have a pair of jeans from Target, Miller says. 'They're starting to want designer labels. They're starting to think that their value increases based on the value of the items they have. So a lot of this has an even deeper impact on girls from lower socio-economic backgrounds who are starting to realise more and more that what our culture defines as attractiveness may be something that they will find very hard to attain. So a lot of young women shoplift.' Girls aged twelve and thirteen – but also as young as ten – are amongst those teens who are caught stealing. 'And I do think sometimes it's their fury at a consumer culture that they find inaccessible,' Miller adds.

A girl's mother also plays a significant role in how her daughter views her body. This observation was repeatedly raised by principals, teachers and psychologists. An irony flares up here, because despite mothers having the power to influence their daughters' view, they also raise their daughter's body image as one of their biggest concerns.

'I just want them to love themselves and their bodies. I don't think I ever thought about my body as good or bad until I was mid teens, and I see them both questioning how they look in the past few years. Very upsetting!'

'Her body esteem awareness has started early with exposure to social media. Her cousins are on TikTok as young as eight [and] always pouting . . . and [she's] complaining she is fat. So sad.'

'I'm surprised at how aware she is about her body. And how concerned she gets if she thinks she's put on any weight. It doesn't affect what she eats, but she talks about her body negatively, which surprises and saddens me.'

'She cried for hours on Sunday night when she got home from dinner at her dad's, as he made six comments about her skirt being too tight and too short. He was probably trying to have a go at me, but she was really hurt and ashamed.'

Mother after mother chronicled how their daughters changed, almost overnight: from dressing in full view to hiding themselves away in their bedrooms like they were ashamed; how they started to skip meals; how they withdrew from ballet soon after making comments about their size or shape; and how they were desperate to have 'skinnier legs'. 'I just want to look different,' one says. 'My biggest worry is my looks,' says another. The reasons were the same all over the country. Pimples marred their face. Braces made them ugly. Their hair was the wrong colour.

Lisa Miller, who heads a junior school in Melbourne, says, 'Body image is closely linked to relationships, and relationships with your mother [in particular], and when those break down due to challenging behaviour . . . that's when you start to see a shift also in body image and self-worth and low self-esteem, because they don't have that positive relationship at home. It's a tricky one,' she says. Sydney principal Paulina Skerman says she has moved to set up a Years 5–6 'tween' precinct at her school as a 'stepping stone' into the more senior years. The emphasis is on staying active and not feeling pressured to behave or appear beyond their years. 'We really want to get kids to value themselves. What they look like is immaterial. It's what's inside.'

The professional advice for parents on how teen body issues should be addressed is almost unanimous. Don't talk about your weight. Don't talk about the weight of others. Talk about how the body functions, not how it looks. Don't talk about food in terms of how it will change the body. Ensure weight is not the subject of jokes in the house. Discourage dieting.

It seems simple, but it's not what is happening in many homes. School principal Kym Amor worries that many mothers talk openly about their weight, and the weight of others, and about what they want to wear or look like. 'It's the risk of what we do as parents, and the things we say and the things we project, that makes a difference. I think that's probably a change from when I was young,' she says. 'My mum was my mum. She didn't want to be anyone else. But I think it's the age group of twenty- to forty-year-old women who are impacting our little girls.' It's a genuine and heartfelt appraisal, and one that is reiterated by others. 'Do not tell your daughters that they are fat; just do not!' says Dannielle Miller. 'There's no reason for that. Also, we've got to understand that, particularly at age ten, their bodies are changing and evolving and they will continue to change and evolve. You don't want to get them to start to examine their bodies forensically. So just don't comment on their size. Their bodies are in a state of flux,' she says.

Miller tells the story of her own daughter coming home from her part-time job at a clothes shop, upset about how a child was being treated by her mother. 'A little girl who was ten had come in with her family and they were looking for a dress for her to wear for her First Holy Communion. And her mother spent the entire time dissecting her daughter's body, saying how fat she looked in this, or did she have anything where they could cover up her arms?' Miller says her daughter saw the ten-year-old's excitement punctured. 'What a tragic thing to do.'

The 2004 movie *Mean Girls* has been seen by most girls, even by the age of ten. Miller knows this because she's asked them. 'It's got a cult following; they love it. Even when they're younger they'll say that they're aware of it,' she says. 'So we remind them of that scene at the end where all of the girls have been arguing and fighting because they've read the awful comments about themselves in the Burn Book. And the teacher asks them to close their eyes, and . . . put their hands up if they've ever said mean things about other girls . . . and all their hands go up.' In workshops, Miller reminds girls of that scene and then explains that she's actually more interested in the things they say about themselves, not others; the words they use with themselves in their inner dialogue – because that's the little voice that won't be silenced. 'We ask them to close their eyes and then we say, hands up if you think you're not a beautiful girl, if you're not as valuable as the other girls, if in some ways you don't measure up. By high school, every girl will put their hand up. It's heartbreaking.

I cry every time ... But with ten-year-olds, I would say it would be about 20 per cent.'

Fathers play an important role here, too, and many raised the issue of how they should discuss a daughter's weight gain with her. The answer? '*Don't.* Don't talk about weight or shape. Shift the focus from appearance to health and other strengths that they have – their personality and who they are as a person, and the function of their body and the things that they're doing,' Tara McLachlan says. Help her to be fit and healthy by encouraging her to go for a walk or a bike ride. And role-model it – alone or, better still, by doing it with her.

Lisa Miller says a significant shift has occurred in the past five years in relation to girls' sexual development. Puberty is arriving earlier than it used to, and personal development lessons that were once delivered in late primary school must now be directed at those in Years 3 and 4.

Sometimes, despite all the work parents put into teaching their daughters about the importance of a healthy body image, their daughter will be unable to escape the messages in circulation. 'I worry about this because we have gone out of our way to never talk about weight, never associate foods with good/or bad labels, and so on,' one mother says. 'We are very aware of the risk factors for eating disorders, and she is already displaying some concerning ideas and behaviours. I worry about this because she seems to be picking up signals about this outside our home.' She wonders whether it might be school, or her daughter's sports club, where she's picked up her views. 'She doesn't have unsupervised internet time, and I don't think she gets it from TV. And I really don't know how to address it in a way that doesn't make it an even bigger deal.'

Taryn Brumfitt, founder of the Body Image Movement, has perhaps done more to address body image than anyone else. Her documentary *Embrace* explores why people hate their bodies and what we can do about it. And it all started after she posted a pair of non-traditional before and after photos of herself (with 'before' being slim and muscular and 'after' being her regular shape) and received 7000 messages of appreciation from people around the globe. Since then, the body positive movement has been growing and educating girls everywhere. 'So is it moving fast enough?' Brumfitt asks. 'No, it never will. But are we getting somewhere? Absolutely we are!'

Hobbies, habits and sport

'Find your own sense of what you like to do and
enjoy it. You have so much to offer everyone.
Girls can get lost in "I want to be, I need to
be like everybody else" as opposed to being
yourself and knowing that you're amazing.'

Joey Peters, former Matilda

How can we teach basketball to children who can't catch? That was the question that prompted Dr Gavin Sandercock and his research team to act. The people asking the question were teachers, and they'd been asking it for several years. So Dr Sandercock, from the University of Essex in England, set about finding out how fit and strong today's ten-year-olds were, and how that might have changed over time. He and his team set about looking at same-aged children, in the same school, year on year. They tested when the children were ten, and again at sixteen, instructing them to undertake a bunch of strength tests, from sit-ups to dangling from monkey bars.

Between 300 and 350 children at schools in the United Kingdom were involved; almost half were girls. All sorts of details were taken, including their height, weight, BMI and waist measurement. Everything was scaled, so children could be compared to those of a decade ago. Dr Sandercock knew, from official data, that ten-year-olds had grown bigger over time, and that more of them were falling into the 'obese' category. But what about fitness? How fast could they run? How strong were they?

The results were fascinating. Girls are 2.5 cm taller than they were sixteen years ago, at the age of ten. This, according to Dr Sandercock, is because puberty was pushing forward by about a month a year in the UK. That meant, on average, many ten-year-olds were pre-pubescent, while others were pubescent. 'We tested them and we scaled it and made it as fair as possible and what we found was that if you think of it pound for pound, kilo for kilo, the kids today – compared to the kids the last time we tested (sixteen years ago) – were a lot weaker.' Their raw strength, on simple things like a pinch grip test, which required no skill or practice, was down 10 to 15 per cent, while their ability on exercise that took effort – like timed sit-ups – was down by 45 per cent! But it was one result that stood out amongst the others. Children were required to hang by their hands from a gym bar, carrying their own weight, holding their legs at a 90 degree angle with their knees bent. They were placed in the position before the instructor stepped back. Says Sandercock, 'That's the only one where we couldn't get them all to do it, because about 30 per cent of the children either refused or simply couldn't do the test. It was dangerous for them to do it because their grip was so poor and their arms were so weak, compared with their body weight, they would just fall off.' Sixteen years ago, every child scored on that test, which was conducted in exactly the same way.

At some schools, researchers had to ask teachers to find the bars because they had been packed away and never used. That told them that children's strength in this area was not being encouraged or tested. But the fact that so many children in this study looked at the bars incredulously and said, 'I can't do that' says as much. 'What about when you climb trees?' Dr Sandercock asked. 'I don't climb trees,' they responded. 'What about when you play on the monkey bars in the park?' Their answer was the same. Says Sandercock, 'It was just something that has been lost, or is becoming lost.' That means many children, at ten, are missing out on the immediate health benefits of being fit and strong and flexible, but it also reduces their ability to join in and participate in sport.

Dr Sandercock's study is seminal to a discussion on hobbies and habits, particularly sport, because this is the age when children often decide to pursue a team sport with more vigour – or drop it. What concerns Sandercock most is the bracket creep evidenced here. The changes are subtle and happen over time, and the infrastructure (like monkey bars) is disappearing from parks at the same time that the rush to climb trees is waning. He says helicopter parenting is a background factor here, and he's experienced that firsthand. 'I've had my kids returned to me from a play park where they were on their own playing,' he says. 'But it's also schools scared of being sued, and as soon as one child falls off an apparatus it is shut down and inspected. It's not the apparatus, it's the kid!' There's one more factor, and that's the screens that are robbing our children of time to play and run and take over our parks. 'In the past twenty years in this country, we've gone from five to 500 TV channels. Nobody at a primary school had ever seen a mobile phone twenty years ago. They certainly didn't have a smartphone. Nearly every new leisure opportunity that's been created for children in the past twenty years involves sitting on your bottom. And, in our day, there was less to do. 'So you found things to do and you created them,' Sandercock says. 'I think that creative play element is lost very young.'

On Dr Sandercock's assessment – and if time travel were possible – a 1 mile (1.6 kilometre) race pitting modern ten-year-olds against their ten-year-old parents would see mums and dads win by about 90 seconds. But diminishing fitness is not a problem isolated to the UK. While Dr Sandercock's research showed almost no difference in fitness levels between the sexes, Australian research has pointed to a disparity between girls and boys. A study by researchers from the University of Canberra and the Australian National University found that eight-year-old girls are less likely to take part in extracurricular sport than boys, and took 2000 fewer steps per day. Overall, girls were 19 per cent less active than boys, had poorer cardio-respiratory fitness and hand–eye coordination, and had a higher percentage of body fat.[1] And for what it's worth, research has also shown that the more active an eleven-year-old girl is, the better she does on standardised school tests in English, Maths and Science.[2]

Ask 500 ten-year-old girls what exercise they love and the answers are delightfully varied. Running. Dance. Netball. Skipping. Basketball. Soccer. AFL. Walking their dog. Gymnastics. Bike-riding. Scooting. Handball. Frisbee. Swimming. Horseriding. Trampolining. Hockey. Skating. Martial Arts. Tennis. But ask them what they most like doing – their favourite pastime – and a sport or activity rarely rates. Art and drawing pop up most, following by 'hanging out with friends'. Then there's sleepovers, reading, Lego, Minecraft, baking, writing stories, having bubble tea, TikTok, anything Harry Potter, eating lollies, singing, playing with their phone. 'I'm really passionate about putting fashion pieces together,' one says. 'And things like make-up, because it makes me feel better.' And: 'I love so much I can't decide!'

Pets registered highly.

'I go to the beach with my dog. I have a Great Dane.'

'I love playing with my dog.'

'Spending time with my puppy, Leo, and horseriding.'

'I LOVE horseriding.'

'I play with my cat.'

'Playing with my parrot.'

Principal Ros Curtis says that pets are everything to children at this age. 'It's an unconditional love, and a constant playmate.' And that's evidenced in boarding schools, where a scan of the walls will show photos of Mum and Dad and siblings . . . and pets galore. 'When a pet dies or something happens to them, we deal with that grief as much as that [for] a family member,' Curtis says.

Screens have taken the place of many hobbies, says psychologist Judith Locke. 'We [as children] had to put colour in our lives. We had to look to stamps. We didn't have a screen. When I was growing up, we only had kids' programming for an hour every afternoon. We had to go and find fun.' She suggests screen-free time for the whole family, regularly. 'I strongly suggest that, because you need the children to be bored to find those passions. The challenge is, when a screen is always available to them they will never seek that kind of activity. It becomes essential for parents to limit screen time so kids do get bored and find other interests.' Many experts suggest screen time is robbing girls of the time they might spend on other activities.

Of course there are exceptions. Children's sewing classes have jumped in popularity in recent years. Music, too, offers a joyful escape for many. Brisbane Regional Youth Orchestra's director, Shaun Dorney, says that while younger girls love the violin and viola, by ten many want to try the flute and clarinet. But at the end of that year, girls tend to lose interest. 'If their friends don't want to do it, they're out.' That friendship factor is crucial. If they remain playing, and join a school ensemble, often it will be with a group of friends who stick together through high school, he says. The benefits went beyond friendship. It expanded their horizons, and even made them more attractive later to employers who valued self-reliance, practice, good time management and the ability to work to a deadline.

Horseriding is another activity that reaps rewards. Dr Kirrilly Thompson, a cultural anthropologist and Pony Club Australia's participation manager, says horseriding offers girls the opportunity to participate in a sport of mixed genders. 'It's also a feeling and a connection and an attraction,' she says. 'I can't think of many other sports where you learn about biology, veterinary stuff, geology and soil quality. Every kind of science and field of learning comes into owning a horse.' Dr Catherine Ainsworth, Pony Club Australia CEO, sees horseriding as having significant impacts on a girl's development. 'Resilience, dealing with things that don't go right the first time, getting dirty, being in nature, having non-school friends of different ages – it's a long list,' she says. Riding a horse provides independence, puts no stock on physical appearance and physique, and helps girls to read signs, communicate in a non-verbal way and build confidence. 'I always talk about the effect of building a relationship – a symbiotic and mutual-understanding relationship – with an animal that could kill you. And I really think that that goes a long way to explaining the impact horses and riding have on the confidence of girls,' she says. It's a world away from the activities many ten-year-olds focus on. 'You get dirty; you fall off and have to get up again; you go away to camp and might not have a shower for three days. There's a lot of that involved in Pony Club.'

It sounds counter-intuitive, teacher and author Daisy Turnbull says, 'to say that the longer you let kids be kids, the better they will "adult", but it is true.' She says the more kids are allowed to 'play in mud, create games and develop their own solutions to problems', the more they will thrive as they grow older. Her comments echo those of Dr Sandercock about parents becoming more risk averse. In her *50 Risks to Take with Your Kids*, Turnbull says, 'Those stories of kids being told to go out and play and come home when the street lights came on are not the stories of twenty- or even thirty-somethings anymore, they are the stories of their grandparents. 'We have generations that have been sheltered from risks, and taught to see the world as an inherently risky place.' Of course the world poses risks, but 'measured, limited and monitored risk-taking for children is one pathway to them becoming resilient, confident adults'.[3]

At the centre of this is the role of 'play', which dips around the age of ten. Sitting around talking at lunchtime becomes more fun than racing around the school yard. Soft toys, which only months earlier for some had been front and centre of games of families or hospitals or schools, might sit more sedentarily on their bed, as do their owners. Former Matilda and Olympian Joey Peters rails against this, saying there should be no age limit on play. 'As adults, it seems foreign, but we should all play – so even more so with children. It's the most important thing in life,' she says. Peters runs a coaching philosophy called Game Play Learn and says play provides an opportunity for children to explore their own capabilities. 'You're gaining confidence in what you can do and that sense of limits and risk in what you can't do,' she says.

The importance of play, early on, is indisputable – it's just that we don't value it as much as our girls grow. One review of evidence found that seeing an activity as play led to both more joy and engagement; that play's social interaction was linked to better learning outcomes; that imaginative play helped children make links to their own knowledge and experience; and that iterative play could lead to more 'creative, innovative ways of thinking and problem solving'.[4] The specific games children choose are not nonsense, either. 'They encourage resilience; they help motor development; and they help children work through their feelings around otherwise unsettling events, like a global pandemic, productively,' says writer Jessica Grose. 'Play is even used as therapy for kids who have lived through monstrous trauma, because it can help children regulate their anxiety, give them a sense of control over their lives and ultimately help them feel safe.'[5] The problem is it often stops abruptly before the age of ten. And without exception, experts consulted on this research bemoaned the 'shortness' of childhood. 'I'd like to think that childhood would go more to twelve and thirteen, rather than begin to wind up at ten,' experienced Adelaide principal Kevin Tutt says. 'I think we should be seeking to delay the end of childhood for as long as possible.'

Phyllis Fagell, author of *Middle School Matters*, says we are largely reaping what we've sown. Society has become more focused on the individual. Our time is too structured. Children no longer have time to play. Extra weight has been put on specific levels of success, like school marks. 'It doesn't leave much wriggle room for kids to fail or to experiment or to just accept themselves for who they are,' she says. If she had her way, children would have a greater voice and more control in families and in schools about what sport they played, what instruments they took up, whether they danced, and when they quit. We'd allow them to try new things, without too much concern for the possible long-term consequences. Parents, especially, find that difficult, but Fagell offers this encouragement: 'I feel as though if we were to give them back some of that autonomy, it would build their self-confidence which would in turn help them self-regulate.' She says some researchers have likened children to prisoners, with parents micro-managing every part of their lives. 'I think all that micro-managing is leaving them with no sense of control over their own destiny, and it's robbing them of confidence.'

The move from simple participation in sport to competitive involvement also plays a role here. 'They are being put in these environments where, rather than being playful, it becomes competitive,' psychologist Karen Young says. 'At ten, it should all be about inclusion.' Even if it's graded, the focus needs to be on a supportive environment that focuses on the whole team. 'If we do that, that's really healthy,' says Young. 'Where it gets tricky is when it is something where they are competing against each other.' This was especially the case because sport, for girls at this age, was largely social. 'So a lot of girls will start sport and keep playing because it's a social thing and it's playful. It's meant to be fun. When it becomes competitive, that stops, and I think a lot of kids leave sport because it stops being fun.'

The developing bodies of some girls rob them of their interest in sport. For example, before ten, most girls will run around a pool in their bathing costume without a second thought. Then at ten and eleven and twelve, and with developing bodies, some will stop. They'll start to 'double tog' – that is, to wear one pair of swimmers over another at school swimming lessons. Others will wear a swim rashie and say that's their parents' rule. Others will feign having their period, knowing a teacher is not going to ask any more questions. Dance is the other area where this happens. While some girls will embrace their tutu proudly, others will stop dancing. 'Dance was something I did when I was little, like nine,' one girl says. 'It doesn't suit me so much now.'

Brisbane principal Ros Curtis raises an interesting point here about sport and fitness, taking issue when I ask about the importance of 'sport', not 'fitness'. 'Fitness has to be really important. Health has to be really important. But it doesn't have to be sport. And it doesn't have to be competitive sport,' she says. She's right – and it's a stellar example of how language is crucial. At the next opportunity, I asked girls whether they played sport. Not everyone did. But they all loved keeping fit – running around with friends, chasing their dog, scooting, going for walks with Mum.

Curtis believes sport and fitness are crucial to girls' wellbeing and body image. And she says competitive sport can also encourage compromise in ten-year-olds. 'You can get a little overconfident sometimes as a young girl, particularly if your parents are always telling you how fantastic you are. And sport can bring you down a peg or two when you realise you're not the best in the netball team,' she says. 'I encourage any girl to remain in competitive sport for as long as possible.' Psychologist Judith Locke believes there should be a rule that all girls play a team ball sport. 'And the reason is because of this plethora of anxiety issues that we're facing right now,' she says. 'A lot of girls with anxiety issues reject ball sports, because they are fearful of dropping the ball, they are fearful of throwing the ball badly, and things like that.' They need to learn how to cope when they make a mistake, or a teammate makes a mistake, or their team loses.

Girls' schools appear successful in keeping ten-, eleven- and twelve-year-olds participating in sport – a fact borne out in studies in several countries showing that girls prefer single-gender PE classes. This doesn't mean that co-ed schools aren't successful, and many are; it is research, however, that highlights the value of girls' schools in this context. Adelaide principal Kevin Tutt says his experience is that girls feel more confident in a single-gender environment.

Ultimately, however, the important thing is to move. Melbourne principal Toni Meath says girls who continue with physical activity through high school carry those learned behaviours into their adult lives, as women. 'So we want them to be as busy and as active as possible,' she says. 'We really want to shift that gaze off their bodies and encourage them to be fit and healthy.'

10

Reaching for the stars

'Self-compassion is the antidote to low
self-esteem. The girls are just so hard on
themselves, and so critical ... Be kind to
yourself and be compassionate to yourself.'

Tara McLachlan, psychologist, Brisbane Girls Grammar School

Run these standardised NAPLAN test questions by your
ten-year-old and listen to her answers.

When the holiday's are over, Dad's uncle (my great uncle)
is coming from Italy to visit.
This sentence contains an error in the use of a
A. capital letter.
B. a comma.
C. an apostrophe.
D. brackets.[1]

*Anna opens a savings account. She deposits $4 in the
first week. She then deposits twice as much money each
week as she did the previous week.*
The total amount of money in the account is
A. always odd.
B. always even.
C. sometimes odd and sometimes even.[2]

Many ten-agers will respond with 'I'm not an English
girl' or 'I'm not a Maths girl' when faced with such questions. In other contexts, we hear ten-year-olds say 'I'm
not a sporty girl'. Throughout this research, I frequently
heard girls tell me what they weren't good at, as if they'd
made up their minds at ten. You can hear psychologist
Karen Young, the founder of the website *Hey Sigmund*,
shudder when she says, 'We don't even know what they're
capable of at ten! They are being put in these environments
where, rather than being playful, it becomes competitive.'
And even when they are told the tests are not competitive,
they are. They're sending signals to children that they are
below par, or not where they should be. 'Even if teachers
and parents are saying, "That's great, you did a great job
and we're really proud of you," they are looking around
them to others,' she says. And if they feel, even in a small
group of four or five friends, that they sit at the bottom in
marks, the message is clear. 'I'm not a smart girl.' 'I'm not
athletic like my friends.' 'I won't be doing Maths/Science

in high school.' They put a ceiling on their potential, and many of them carry that forward into Years 6 and 7. 'We don't even know at ten what they'll be like,' Karen Young says. 'Their brains are still developing.'

In this project, I chased so many rabbits down so many holes: girls' passion for their pets; their love of cooking; how they wanted to make the world a better place; their struggle with finding enduring friends; what they see when they look into the mirror; the messages encrypted in the digital wallpaper that fills their lives; the first tentative steps of independence; the brutality delivered by COVID-19; the anguish of depression, self-harm and eating disorders; the search for self-esteem and the monster that body image sometimes presents. But the one that got me in the pit of my stomach was how ten-year-olds are determining what they see as their future path . . . in Year 5! Many of them then author their own story going forward. They stop trying in a particular subject. They withdraw from the hockey team. They decide the science club is not for them – it's for the 'science girls'.

'I can't do Maths.'

'I'm not good at sport.'

'I can never get my homework done on time.'

'I worry about school work because I'm not good at it.'

'I am bad at school stuff.'

'I worry about not being able to go to high school because I'm not smart enough.'

What these girls aren't recognising is that the skill and interests they have at ten are not indicative of the path they will follow (and they need to believe that!), and that what they believe they are not good at is a tiny slice of life's pie. None of them say they are not good at being kind, or having empathy, or playing an instrument, or sewing, or debating, or being a pet owner, or any number of other talents that can be just as important, if not more important, than a Year 5 Maths quiz.

'My daughter thinks because she isn't getting As at school, she's not smart,' one Mum wrote to me. 'I find that sad.' Another says this: 'She can't even ride a bike, and now she will no longer try.' Another: 'She's given up on sport because she has a high standard and doesn't believe she's any good.' And yet another: 'She won't make the most of her talents because she is terrified of making mistakes or looking foolish.' And so it goes on – a fear that girls are pigeonholing themselves at the age of ten and eleven.

'She thinks she's not good at Maths.'

'She limits her potential by not believing she is capable of improving.'

'I'm concerned that she quickly thinks she isn't good enough academically.'

'I hate this comparison culture she's growing up in.'

'She feels she's not good at anything and it doesn't help that she has a very academic older sister and a very athletic older brother.'

These comments touch on just a few of many issues that need to be discussed, including the role of mixed-ability or streamed classrooms, the type of school you choose for your daughter, the role a sibling can play in how a ten-year-old sees herself, the driving instant gratification many of our children need, and the lack of perseverance that now marks many of their activities. One mother says that more than anything she wants her ten-year-old to learn to 'stick things out more so that she can get really good at something'. 'She does tend to give up easily and say she's not good at it rather than put in the hard work. She's given up all extracurricular activities because of this, and she has tried a lot.'

Professor Susan Sawyer, president of the International Association of Adolescent Health, says those limitations can be the result of gendered views of what boys and girls should or could do in families. But potential is also being limited by what, at this age, girls internalise. 'This is often very unconscious, but we take on board the values around us and the feedback we get as being either successful or not successful,' she says. That can affect the confidence we then have in engaging in tasks – like Maths. And our confidence and expectations will shape how 'brave' we will be in terms of future engagement. 'I was eight when my Maths teacher said I was hopeless at Maths,' school counsellor Marcelle Nader-Turner says, 'And my mother said, "Oh yes, she's just like me. I was never good at Maths either." So, you know, I was never going to be good at Maths because I wasn't good at Maths.' Karen Spiller, principal of John Paul College in Brisbane, says it never helps when parents reinforce that they struggled with a subject. She says girls need female role models who are successful across disciplines. 'Not the dorky scientist in the white lab coat,' she says. 'They need . . . role models who can inspire them to give it a go – nothing ventured, nothing gained.'

The tendency of young girls – and, often inadvertently, their parents – to put a ceiling on their talents frustrates educators the length and breadth of our nation. The principal of Korowa Anglican Girls' School in Melbourne, Helen Carmody, sees this journey, for many girls, as part of their search for identity. They take on the messages of those around them, and that can quite quickly deliver very closed options for themselves. Carmody, and almost everyone else canvassed, raises the issue of whether we might compliment our children too much. 'I think parents tell them a lot of what they're good at. You know, rather than rewarding them for the work that they do, or for the challenges that they face, or the things they try, there is that whole constant praise thing,' she says. It sounds like this: 'Oh, that's beautiful artwork, but then you're such a wonderful artist.' Rather than: 'You worked so hard. You must be proud of that; it took ten hours.' Author Rebecca Sparrow says, 'That idea of "you are amazing" and "look how amazing you are" – that message I think is problematic. And when you have that message, I think maybe you have less room for understanding [others].'

Matt Macoustra, deputy head (operations) at Sydney's Barker College, says that if you ask a girl why she says she's 'not a Maths person' she'll say, 'Because I'm not good at it.' Sometimes he sees the penny drop when he explains that perseverance can change that. 'And it seems to be far more prevalent with young women than it is with boys,' he says. Girls could sometimes internalise criticism and take an exam result personally, rather than see it as 'a mark on the page'. He provides this analogy: if a boy was told he had made a mistake at football, he'd think he didn't kick the ball well in that particular match; it would not become an issue about him as a person. A girl, however, would be likely to take the mistake personally. In another sporting analogy, Macoustra describes the mindset of a cricket player. A positive player will look for the gaps between the fielders and decide that's where they'll hit the ball. 'Whereas the person mired in a negative mindset is thinking, "Look at where all those people are standing" and, "Where am I going to hit this ball?" It's such a subtle difference, but if you apply that to a school situation, a kid with the growth mindset is going to look at it and say, "I'm really strong in a whole lot of these areas and I'm going to have a red hot go at this", whereas the other is going to say, "Look at Question 10; that's so hard. I'll never be able to do that."' And as a result, their performance suffers.

Author of *Middle School Matters*, Phyllis Fagell, says sometimes parents jump in to provide children with a more positive assessment than they should. 'For example, if a ten-year-old says they can't run fast, a parent might get them to remember the time in Year 2 when they got second in a race,' she says. That does two things. First, children – who are aware that their parents are biased – feel 'invalidated'. Fagell tells parents to pause and ask themselves whether what they are about to say is 'inside their child's control or outside their child's control'. 'It's important to comment on what they can control – their bravery, tenacity, resilience, et cetera.' The second thing to remember is that our own journey wasn't linear; we made mistakes, had to regroup, and that wasn't always easy. Our children need to hear that, she says. 'To kids of eleven, parents are still heroes. It might seem as though they don't care what we think, but they very much do care what we think.'

Miami State High School principal Susan Dalton says the limits girls put on themselves are often related to academic results. 'I think in Grade 6 they really label themselves and pigeonhole themselves to a profile that fits an education group, and in my mind it is too early, way too early.' Dr Toni Meath, the principal of Melbourne Girls Grammar School, says she tells her Year 5 and 6 students what she wants of them: 'We want you to be wild. We want you to explore. We want you to be curious. And we want you to play.' The school's Wildfell program, for that age group, aims to bridge primary and secondary education. The girls come to the school's senior campus, where they access secondary Science and Maths and Art and Language teachers. 'So they actually have their class-room teacher like any primary-level child would, but we give them all of the electives and the specialist teachers – teachers who teach all the way up to Year 12. We really look at those two years as foundational for their confidence for the rest of their secondary schooling,' she says. Dr Meath, who has headed several schools, says focused effort is also, at this time, put into spelling, grammar and rote learning of times tables, to build confidence.

Educators say that if a child has made up their mind they can or can't do something, it's difficult to shift that mindset. It's prompted some schools to cross subjects – for example, to include Art in Science, or Technology in Maths. 'So the learning comes together so you can see the application of what you're doing and think less about things being compartmentalised along subject lines,' one educator says. Another explains an early entrepreneurship focus, where children are encouraged to create a product, pitch it, sell it and create a business plan. The idea, from beginning to end, is to open closed minds. Susan Dalton says schools need to be strategic with their timetabling, to provide girls with a smorgasbord of experiences so that they don't narrow down their interests and abilities too early. 'Schools do have control over how they can help facilitate not pigeonholing girls at that age,' she says. But constant work has to be done to ensure that girls continue to 'reach for the stars', step out of their comfort zones and be part of a 'culture of inclusion'. It works best when parents and the school engage together. So what advice would Dalton give those parents whose girls are wobbly over continuing activities they don't win at? To listen more than we talk. Keep the lines of communication open. And don't use our daughters to fulfil our own dreams.

Sydney principal Paulina Skerman sees girls limiting their potential as part of a drive towards perfectionism: '"If I can't do that one hundred per cent, I won't have a go at all." I think they start to become afraid of failing.' This behaviour is fascinating. Skerman observes that as girls become women, often a 'brake' is activated. 'So we go from these carefree girls to women, and maybe pick up on all those insecurities of the women they know.' The difference here with boys, generally, is well recognised. They will push themselves out to the front. Girls will be more reluctant. 'A boy will say he can do it before he's even had a go, whereas a girl, if she can't do it properly, won't have a go at all,' Skerman says. This same issue is a passion for Brisbane principal Ros Curtis, who agrees that girls form views on their ability in Maths and Science far too early. Her belief is that our daughters are limiting their potential in pursuit of always being happy. 'I think we've applied this thing in society that says you're meant to be happy. That means you're in no discomfort. Whereas we've never been given the proper message, which is: it's great if you're happy *on balance*,' she says. When this is explained to others, they quickly agree. As parents, we are looking for our children to be happy every single minute of the day. 'And that's not how it works,' Curtis says. Indeed, big achievements can be gained by putting ourselves outside of our comfort zones.

It's only a very small jump from the pursuit of happiness to the pursuit of perfectionism, Curtis believes. 'So what you start to find is that girls think they have to be perfect, and that shows itself at school.' This might mean, for example, that a child will not hand in work where they have been forced to cross something out. They can't present it because it's not 'perfect'. The next step is that if they believe they can't complete it perfectly, they don't. 'So they don't hand in work,' Curtis says. 'Then [they] can say to [themselves], "I didn't get good marks because I didn't do it" – not because I did it and it wasn't up to standard. So, happy and perfect are a problem.' She tries to address it in a routine way in the school grounds by asking children how they are feeling. One might say, 'I'm okay, I guess,' and she will respond with, 'You don't sound very happy.' She continues: 'They'll say, "Well I'm not really happy today" and I'll say, "Good, because you don't have to be happy every day. I hope it improves for you, but you don't have to be [happy all the time]. I wasn't happy yesterday but I'm okay today."' And then she moves on. School counsellor Tara McLachlan says the pursuit of 'effortless perfectionism' is a big issue. 'The pressure to succeed and have academic success, but also manage to be attractive, fit, well-dressed and have the right friends, without showing any visible effort – this leads to the girls being overcommitted and putting immense pressure on themselves to be exceptional in all of their endeavours,' she says. Girls are also likely to ruminate and focus on their distress.

Brisbane school principal Catherine O'Kane says global connectivity means the comparison pool is now limitless; girls can access comparisons with peers across the globe. 'It's around the messaging we give to the girls. So stop comparing yourself to everybody else. Find joy in things that you find joy in and don't let it worry you that other people don't find joy in it. The other things will come.'

This makes choosing a school a crucial decision, because one may suit a particular child and really not suit another. The best education for ten-year-olds differs, according to the experts. Some principals believe students rise by putting them at the lower end of high school. Others say their leadership blossoms when they are the eldest in a primary school setting. And many maintain that a middle school environment allows them to grow at their own pace. Unsurprisingly, those who run all-girls schools say the battle to determine self-identity is more easily won when they are surrounded by female peers. Dr Toni Meath says girls will try more activities when they are separated from boys. 'There's no lens there of bias, and there's no requirement for them to be anything but themselves,' she says. 'Because even at the age of ten, the boys will take up space and they'll speak first and the girls will try and please and do the right thing and step back and compromise themselves. In a girls' school, they just all muck in and do it themselves.' In her view, parents should seek for their daughters a calm, happy school that focuses on relationships. And consider what the graduates of the school look like.

The transition from primary to middle or high school weighs on girls' minds, and the minds of their parents.

They worry about what they see as the competitive nature of some private schools, 'where there are mental health issues and a race to get perfect grades'. They worry that a big school, in which she would be one of hundreds and hundreds, would dim their daughter's personality. They worry that she will not meet the right friends, or be able to keep up with the workload, or be lost in a system that doesn't always favour the quirky. While girls' schools are strongly encouraged by many, a big chunk of parents maintain that having boys in the class defuses female friendship issues.

So how do most parents choose a school?

'We decided on a smaller private school because we think it has better pastoral care.'

'It is a girls-only school and we believe they have a strong program for developing girls into strong women/leaders/ being the best they can be.'

'An all-rounder co-ed school within walking distance of home.'

'We've chosen an all-girls school as I think this could be good for female empowerment.'

'I wanted her to have a nurturing environment from a wellbeing perspective.'

'We have chosen a well-rounded school that is not just focused on academics.'

'She will go to a co-ed school in Year 7. I think it is a snippet of the real world.'

'Because she was very quiet as a child, and shy, and the best place for her was a private girls' school with a reputation for a nurturing environment.'

'It has a wonderful ethos of encouraging girls to be "the best they can be", which the principal went to great pains to explain is something different for every girl.'

'The high school we have decided on provides options in extracurricular areas that might assist with her finding her tribe and not getting lost in a sea of faces.'

Taking out factors like geography and sibling attendance, the three most dominant motivating forces for choosing a school were finding a single-gender or co-ed school based on their perceived values, the school's size and its focus on wellbeing. In my survey of 1600 parents, these factors played a bigger role than a choice based on where a parent went to school, what the fees were, who led a school, the subject choices available and religion. What confused parents were the different ways of dealing with this age group. 'Are they better in a primary school, as leaders, or as the babies in a high school?' was a commonly asked question.

Phyllis Fagell says the focus should not be on whether an educational institution is called a middle, junior or high school. 'Take away that label of a structure and create a structure that serves their unique needs,' she says. She advocates home rooms, the same teachers for most subjects and changing schools when a child is most ready. Her suggestions don't stop there. 'I would get rid of all the standardised testing, which is useless . . . and do what I could in the school setting to give them opportunities.' Opportunities like mixing with other children, a greater say in how to raise funds and how to spend them, even the chance to join school interview committees. Girls, she says, need to be 'the expert in their own life'.

Sometimes the school might be right for your friend's daughter but not your own. One mum, who works with children, visited that learning curve with her own daughter. She chose a small school. 'The great thing about a small school is that you're always seen,' she says. 'The bad thing about a small school is that you're always seen . . . and she [her daughter] felt that pressure. She felt you had to be known for something. Because she's very academic, she felt completely boxed in.' So she moved her to another school. 'I said to her [that] I wanted her to be at a place that does school musicals and I want her to do cooking and I want her to know that being academic is one thing.

There's so much more that you are and that you should be exposed to.' The point is that different schools suit different children. In this case, the mother learnt that her daughter needed a big school. 'She's shy and prefers a bigger school because there's the freedom to try things without all eyes on you.'

Once inside the school, the teachers and teaching methods can 'make or break' a student, according to one expert. Paul Dillon, who works with school communities around alcohol and drugs, says that where teachers used to be masters of a subject, now they are experts on children. 'That's a big change that has occurred,' he says. 'What makes you a great Physics teacher is that you can connect with the kids and have a great relationship with them.' Relationships are paramount. 'You can have the best educated kids, the kids who know their alphabet backwards and know the times table, but if they're not coping with the world and they don't have a good relationship with others . . .' His voice trails off – but teachers agree. One mother, who is also a teacher, explains it with her own tween daughter. 'When there's a beautiful connection between the teacher and the child and the teacher sees the child for who she is and accepts her for who she is, and sees her strengths and helps her to build on those – but also sees her areas for growth as opportunities, not a problem – it makes a real difference.'

If the match isn't right, it can have an impact on both the girl's self-esteem and her learning.

A final point here on learning, raised over and over by teachers, that goes back to the heart of ten-year-old girls limiting their potential. Many of those surveyed believe 'mixed-ability classrooms' create anxiety, and encourage girls to self-assess – to their detriment. 'The student at the top of the class is a constant reminder to the struggling students,' one says. Now some schools stream, some schools 'bank' students (a softer form of streaming) and some run mixed-ability classes. It's not black or white. Educational leaders believe that streaming can help girls academically. Some advocate it, others rail against it. Teachers admit they teach 'to the middle of the class', which can help lift some girls in mixed-ability classes. At the end of the day, though, it's just another factor in encouraging our girls to push through that ceiling of potential and reach for their own stars – not those carrying someone else's name.

Anxiety and mental health

'Make talking about feelings and emotions the
most normal thing there is. Make home a place at
age ten – and well before that – where anything
can be discussed without judgement or ridicule.'

Marcelle Nader-Turner, school counsellor, St Hilda's
Collegiate School, Dunedin, New Zealand

Ask more than 500 ten-year-old girls what worries
them most and the answers cover the spectrum, from
snakes coming out of sinks to giant moths, from kidnap-
pers arriving at school to escaped murderers breaking into
their bedrooms. Perhaps we were no different at their
age. The dark has always been scary for many. So has the
news, which is now more accessible than ever. But other
fears popped up so many times it's worth delving into
the worries that are turning smiles into too many frowns.

The death of a pet came up almost as much as the illness or death of a parent. The judgement of friends frequently registered as a worry. Fighting between parents understandably unsettled a child of any age. The amount and difficulty of schoolwork was nominated by almost one-fifth of all ten-year-olds. And concern about physical features – particularly weight and height – came up disturbingly often (see Chapter 8). But so did other issues. Consider these examples:

'I worry about many things, mostly everything, but especially bad grades and my family getting mad.'

'I worry about missing too much of Year 6 because of the coronavirus.'

'I worry about people not liking me and what others think of me.'

'Being the odd one out in a friendship group or at a party.'

'I worry about when my parents fight.'

'My grades; I'm worried I won't have good enough grades to become a doctor ... and then fail in school.'

'My family dying.'

'My dog dying.'

'I'm too tall.'

'I'm too tall to be ten.'

'I'm worried because I'm not thin.'

'If I could take someone from my family [with me] when I die it would be my dog.'

Lisa Miller, head of a Melbourne junior school, understands the importance of pets. 'That's their real love,' she says. And it was the same when she was ten. 'I remember my first love was my dog, and when he got run over by a car in front of me I cried for days. My heart was broken.' Worry about the death of a pet is understandable, as is worry (for some children) about anaphylaxis, not fitting in, exams and sick parents. But most fears were less rational, or the situations in which they might occur quite remote: giant spiders sitting on their face; whether airbags in cars would work when needed; crocodiles; the pain of giving birth. The Australian Institute of Family Studies (AIFS) warns against trivialising our children's concerns. 'It is important to understand what children and young people worry about in order to support them to deal with these concerns effectively, so that they do not become overwhelming and negatively affect their mental health,' a 2018 AIFS report says.[1] Based on the Longitudinal Study of Australian Children (LSAC), it says research indicates that the more worries a child has, the more likely they are to become anxious or depressed.[2]

The views of the 500 ten-year-old girls who contributed to this book typified those raised in the AIFS study, which found that worrying about the health of family members was the most common concern for children aged ten to eleven: 'Two in three ten- to eleven-year-olds said that they were worried about a family member becoming seriously ill or injured'. Additionally, 'more than half were concerned about fighting within their family, and more than four in 10 children were worried about their parents losing their job,' the report says. That research, based on ten-year-olds in 2014, found that girls worried more than boys, and the biggest difference related to worries about how they looked and fitted in with friends. 'The only issue that concerned boys more than girls was the possibility that one of their parents may lose their job – almost half (49 per cent) of boys indicated that they worried about this aged ten to eleven, compared to 42 per cent of girls,' the AIFS report says. It also found that children from less advantaged families worried more about a range of issues than those from more advantaged families, and that parental education had a more widespread influence on children's worries at ages ten and eleven than parental income. Children from culturally and linguistically diverse (CALD) families also worried more than children from non-CALD families.[3]

The space of years between the 2014 LSAC research and this project revealed one issue on which there was a divergence. In just six years, a new worry might be occupying our girls' minds. The AIFS report had noted that how girls looked and whether they fitted in with their friends were issues of only limited concern to children: one-fifth of them worried about how they looked and one-quarter were concerned about how they fitted in. But in my project, those two issues – fitting in and appearance – loomed larger, almost dominating the worries of girls in schools across Australia. Young, healthy girls readily labelled themselves too tall, too small, too fat, too shy, boring, uninteresting and unable to find others like them.

Parents are certainly alert to the growing worries and anxiety taking hold amongst their children. And certainly it is an issue of great concern in schools containing this cohort. Almost every principal raised it. Almost every school counsellor raised it. Counsellers say that, for a ten-year-old, anxiety can be a growing worry, a genuine concern, sometimes about something even far in the future. It can feel like sickness has invaded the pit of their stomach, or a feeling of dread. And it can be seen in avoidance too: avoidance of tasks, of assessments, of classes and of school. (Indeed, some schools found that school avoidance – where a child simply would not go – jumped during the return-to-school following the first wave of COVID-19.)

Children, too, didn't hesitate to name the worries that occupied their thoughts, and their parents nominated their children's anxiety as the issue on which they most wanted help.

> 'She has an obsessive fear of my death – especially when I travel for work. She is utterly convinced that I will die THIS TIME. Nothing can be done to dissuade her.'

> 'She has said things like "I hate myself sometimes", which worries me constantly.'

> 'She has struggled with anxiety (sometimes it would take two hours for her to get into a headspace that she could walk into school) through primary school.'

> 'As she gets older my biggest fear is her mental health. I can protect her from so many things in life and give her the skills to make good choices, but my biggest fear is how I can protect her mental health as she gets older.'

Gender identity and sexual identity were also raised by several parents as other issues their ten-year-olds are anxious about. 'She's questioning whether she's gay or bi before ever having kissed someone,' one says. 'Her best friend at school told their circle of friends she was bi, spurring [my daughter's] mind into action to question her [own] preference.' While questioning these things may be a natural step in a child's growth, it is concerning if it develops into a source of anxiety for our ten-agers. One mother mentioned her own fears around how her child would be accepted: 'I'm scared every day. As a mother even more so now I have a transgender child.' Other parents reported their daughters coming home asking what the terms 'transgender' and 'bi' meant, pointing again to that huge gulf between the worlds of different ten-year-olds.

Kevin Tutt, who has headed several schools including Adelaide's Seymour College, says he's seen the level of anxiety in ten-year-olds grow exponentially over recent years. 'The issues are what most young teenagers have had to deal with, they're just dealing with it at an earlier age, and it's things like friendships, relationships, boys, physical appearance – all those things that teenagers have always gone through,' he says. Toni Riordan, who runs St Aidan's Anglican Girls' School in Brisbane, labels anxiety as her biggest concern. She sees it as a product of two changes. First, girls are developing faster, and second their access to information has made them more worldly. 'And as a result I think they ask questions at a very young age, which could very well be developing anxiety, essentially because there is this access to information that in previous generations would have been for older children to adults. They now have the access, and are trying to understand it.'

Tara McLachlan is school psychologist for Brisbane Girls Grammar School. There, girls are interviewed at around age ten to take their place in Year 7. As in most other schools, anxiety is the 'biggest presenting issue'.

McLachlan nominates many factors that may be contributing to this, including separated families who do not work together and the pervasive influence of social media. Once upon a time, children could leave school and their friendship woes at the school gate each afternoon, knowing home offered a sanctuary. 'But now at home they're still communicating with friends, so it is a continuation from the playground.'

Professor James Scott, a psychiatrist who leads the Child and Youth Research Group at the QIMR Berghofer Medical Research Institute, regularly sees children with the kinds of worries raised by the 500 ten-year-old girls in this project. He says a difference exists between boys and girls. 'These are generalities, but in general, girls are much more thoughtful of what others say and think about them than boys are. They worry about what their friends and peers say about them. They worry more about what teachers think about them, what their parents think about them.' And he's seen the exponential growth in anxiety, too. 'I think there's much more of an awareness of the need to do well academically, particularly for girls. They worry a lot more about schoolwork and how they perform. When we [as children] did a Maths quiz, we didn't think much of it,' he says. 'We just did it. But now these things have become a big deal.' He says it's partly driven by parental expectations, along with kids being aware of what is expected of them later in life and how success is seen. And it is the 'burden' presented by that worry that concerns him most.

The role parents play, without even realising it, is climacteric, and many school principals referred to the pressure some parents unwittingly place on their daughters. 'You should be having the right friendships, and doing this extracurricular activity, and getting this result, and wearing these clothes,' one principal says. Rebecca Sparrow reports that she has been at primary school swimming carnivals where parents are sitting with stopwatches and notebooks and the first thing they say to their child when they come out of the water is, 'What happened? Your turn was slow.' It's the same with exam results and report cards. 'Wouldn't it be wonderful to see the girls able to explore those things for themselves, without feeling like they need to fit the mould,' a Sydney principal says. And this from a peer educator in Melbourne: 'In a single class of twenty-four girls, we will have five or six girls . . . who are being treated for anxiety,' she says. 'I think parents do play a big role here. Rather than giving [their girls] strategies to deal with it, some almost feed it. Let's deal with it. Let's actually give them . . . some strategies for how they can solve it and manage it themselves.'

So what is the best way to deal with anxiety? What other mental health issues are knocking at the classroom door? And how can you best protect your daughter from the heartache anxiety can bring? 'Just validate their feelings,' school psychologist Tara McLachlan says. 'I think that's the most important thing to do. Listen to them; talk about their worries; don't dismiss them. Don't say, "Don't worry about it, it's fine." Make them feel heard and understood. I think that's just so important.' That's her advice to parents and guardians. What about to ten-year-olds themselves? 'I would name the feeling, because sometimes they don't have a name for it,' she says. The 'Name It to Tame It' strategy was developed by psychiatrist and author Dr Daniel Siegel, and McLachlan says it allows girls to understand what they might be experiencing. 'I talk to them about how their bodies are really good at detecting threat. And that's because their ancestors were really good at surviving,' she says. It is also important for girls to realise that we all suffer degrees of anxiety and that certain strategies can stop it 'tipping over into the unhelpful zone'.

Experts everywhere give similar advice about anxiety: recognise it, acknowledge it, deal with it. Dealing with it might require medical intervention, but Beyond Blue also recommends ten anxiety-management strategies for people of all ages. These involve slow breathing, progressive muscle relaxation, learning to stay in the present moment (perhaps with meditation), focusing on lifestyle factors (like diet, sleep and exercise), taking small acts of bravery, challenging negative self-talk, planning worry time, getting to know your anxiety, learning from others and being kind to yourself.[4]

Educator Lisa Miller says parents and teachers need to work together to make our children feel safe. 'We have to teach our kids to be mindful and to practise mindfulness habits; to learn that early and to learn about meditation and calming the mind,' she says. At many schools, children aged ten are provided with mindfulness and meditation sessions. 'We seem to have shifted into this rapid pace ... This whole process of "I've got to keep up, I've got to keep going" – children don't need that.' Miller, like her peers, highlights the important of learning through play. Brisbane principal Ros Curtis says that maintenance of a routine helps to curb anxiety. She gives the example of online learning during COVID shutdowns. Her school made the conscious decision to follow its regular timetable, 'so that they knew exactly where they should be on a Tuesday at 12:20 pm,' she says. Routine eased many students' anxiety.

While anxiety is the most common issue school psychologists deal with, eating disorders and self-harm are making inroads. 'The diagnosis of an eating disorder once might not have happened until senior school,' one school counsellor says, 'but we are now seeing it earlier and earlier.' Professor Susan Sawyer, president of the International Association of Adolescent Health, says there is no evidence that anorexia nervosa is in decline. 'We see very similar incidence rates [to those] we've seen over many years. My personal belief – and I have no evidence to support it – is that we're seeing probably less bulimia nervosa. And I have certainly wondered whether the epidemic of self-harm is a mechanism which has taken over from that,' she says.

As discussed in Chapter 7, Hugh van Cuylenberg authored *The Resilience Project*, a book about (as its subtitle indicates) finding happiness through gratitude, empathy and mindfulness. Part of van Cuylenberg's motivation for writing that book was to try to understand the mental health abyss his sister, Georgia, fell into when she was young. He says he meets so many other young 'Georgias' when he speaks at schools. With mental health problems affecting 40 per cent of all Australian high school students, he suspects he's met 'thousands'. 'At the last girls' school I spoke at, I finished the talk ... in a room of about 300, I probably had thirty waiting to have a chat to me.' Each of those has a family, and friends, caught up in a mental health maze. 'A girl might come up and talk to me after a session but then I think about her parents and her siblings and I just know they're all going through it – a ripple effect that touches so many other people.'

This is not an Australian-only problem. American writer Phyllis Fagell says language, in dealing with ten-year-old girls, is vital. In the US, she explains during our interview, schools adopted a pass–fail mark during COVID. Students only passed or failed assessments, no specific mark or percentage was given. Fagell had talked about this with one unhappy young girl. She relates their conversation: 'She is incredibly hard on herself and to the point it is interfering with her sleep, and I said, "I'm curious if the fact that it is pass–fail has had a positive effect on your stress levels, because it seems as though you're still pretty stressed. And she said to me, "It's worse. It's the language. It's the word 'fail'. If it's pass or fail, there's really nothing in between."' Fagell says she had never considered that, and authorities soon changed it from 'fail' to 'incomplete'. In her work, two issues dominate. 'In the US between 2007 and 2014, the suicide rate among ten- to fourteen-year-olds doubled,' she says. 'I think ten-year-olds have a very hard time knowing how they feel; it's not normal for them to ask for help.' Her other major concern was born of US research showing that the confidence levels of girls aged between eight and fourteen dropped 30 per cent. 'Confidence that other people like them in that same age range drops 46 percent,' she said. 'We have this combination of spiking mental health issues coupled with plummeting self-confidence.' Other studies give rise to the same concerns. Indeed, a University of Queensland global study of mental health in 2020 found that about one in five teens experienced thoughts of suicide or anxiety. That study investigated data collected from more than 275,000 adolescents aged twelve to seventeen years across eighty-two low-, middle- and high-income countries and found 14 per cent had had suicidal thoughts and 9 per cent suffered anxiety over a twelve-month period.[5]

Self-harm was mentioned fleetingly above and deserves focused attention. It is increasing, and those doing it are becoming younger and younger. Most young girls are not self-reporting. Often it's a peer or a member of a sports department who has noticed unusual marks on a student (say, while wearing a swimming costume or the school sports uniform). And sometimes it is parents who notice – like the couple who spotted marks high on the thigh of their daughter during school holidays, or the mother who found two razor blades, in a pack, deep inside her daughter's shoe. Several counsellors raised it as the new challenge. Sometimes the girls knew why they were doing it, sometimes they didn't. But usually, counsellors say, it is about regulating their emotions: girls can tend to internalise, and self-harm can become a coping mechanism. All warned against believing it was a particular 'type' of girl who self-harmed, and gave cases of anxious girls, those who were depressed and others with low self-worth. 'There's different functions of self-harm and so you get girls presenting with different reasons,' one counsellor says. 'For some it might be more than one reason, too.' In all cases, those interviewed recommended professional support.

Finally, a warning from Karen Young, psychologist and founder of the popular website *Hey Sigmund*. She warns against 'pathologising' too much when we talk about anxiety. 'Anxiety's always been there,' she says. 'So there's this idea that if I'm scared of something or if I'm worried or if I'm anxious, there's something wrong with me. That drives anxiety about the anxiety.' It becomes a vicious cycle. '"Am I broken? What's wrong with me, because I shouldn't be feeling like this." You feel like that because you do. And of course, it gets to a level where it gets in the way.' Young's advice for girls is practical, and largely implementable. Play a game. Sleep. Have some more sleep. Watch what you eat. 'We find kids eating more processed foods, or not eating enough, restricting their diet or not getting everything they need – that's going to play into their mental health,' she says. And remember that anxiety exists on a spectrum from 'normal worry' to 'big worry'.

It might be understandable that a ten-year-old, especially at a new school, is anxious about going to camp or trying something new, or in some cases even going to school. 'What we need to be careful of is how we talk to kids about it,' Young says. Sometimes she hears parents talk in a way that suggests 'there is something wrong' with their children. 'And yes, if it is intrusive, and it's getting in the way, that's a problem. But the more we talk about it to kids as a problem, the more they're going to say, "I'm the problem".' Young says adults needed to show leadership in dealing with it, by explaining that new challenges can be trying. 'But this isn't about how strong she is, or how brave she is, or how capable she is. It's got nothing to do with that.' Teachers get anxious too, Young reminds us. Everybody does. 'I don't want to belittle anxiety at all,' she says. 'I don't want to minimise it. If it gets in the way, it can drive self-harm. It can drive addiction.' But anxiety itself isn't the problem; it is what it feeds into: friendships and homework, class tasks and trying new adventures. The lives of ten-year-olds.

12

Popular culture

'[I wish] they would allow themselves to
play, to care less about how they look,
and more importantly be less concerned
about how others think of them.'

Year 5 teacher

Anni-Frid Lyngstad stole my heart when I was ten. But it was Agnetha Fältskog who my friends thought I emulated. Anni-Frid had the wild hair, and that put me squarely in her corner. But it didn't matter too much, because we all loved everything about ABBA. We were too young to contemplate seeing them during their whirl-wind 1977 tour, but it didn't stop us singing into our hairbrushes and dancing away lunch hours. We were all Dancing Queens. The Bay City Rollers weren't far behind them in our estimation. Perhaps the first boy I looked at was Derek Longmuir, their drummer, whose photograph popped up in my diary a touch too frequently under the headline, 'I Only Wanna Be With You'. But it was their tartan attire that grabbed my attention even more, and it didn't matter a scrap that it trapped every ounce of the burning western Queensland heat. *The Brady Bunch* was big, too, and a spot of envy was directed at Cindy Brady with her delightful curls and naughty smile. It was inspirational; I remember thinking that one day my family might have a self-deprecating housekeeper like Alice Nelson. Tidying my room would be someone else's job.

Full House, the American sitcom, and its Netflix sequel, *Fuller House*, might be the modern-day *Brady Bunch*, which had widowed architect Mike Brady join with Carol Martin and their combined six children. In *Full House*, a widowed dad raises his three daughters with the help of his rock'n'roll brother-in-law and best friend. When ten-year-old girls are asked about their favourite television show or movie, *Full House* triumphs. Of course there are others – from *Tiger King* to *9-1-1*, *Outer Banks* to *SpongeBob SquarePants*, *Bondi Rescue* to *Stranger Things*. *The Next Step, Friends, Horrible Histories, Brooklyn Nine-Nine, Stuck in the Middle, Haters Back Off, H2O: Just Add Water, Pitch Perfect, Lego Masters* and *MasterChef Australia* were also wildly popular, according to the 500 girls canvassed for this project. The top three – *Fuller House, Lego Masters* and *MasterChef* – are all different,

but all upbeat and inclusive. And that in itself says something delightful about this gorgeous group of Generation
Alphas. *Fuller House* gets votes because of its humour
and the fact that it's about everyday life, and Kimmie –
the annoying neighbour – is an unlikely inspiration for
many girls. *MasterChef* is about 'normal' Australians
who boast spectacular cooking ability. Ten-year-old girls
love the competitive nature of the show as much as the
culinary creations that fill the screen. Some have used it
as an inspiration to write their own cookbooks, which
they've published online.

Our ten-year-olds' interest in books is as varied as
the group itself. Firm favourites are unsurprising. Harry
Potter. Enid Blyton, particularly *The Naughtiest Girl
in the School*. The Friday Barnes series. *Wings of Fire*.
The Hobbit. The Land of Stories series. Scarlet and
Ivy. *The Diary of Anne Frank*. The Percy Jackson series.
Ice Wolves. The Babysitter's Club. Dork Diaries. *Keeper
of the Lost Cities*. David Walliams's books. *The Hunger
Games*. The list runs to pages, but two themes are clear:
a variance in reading ability and interest, and the fact that
almost every child nominated a book. Only a handful
were not reading. This, too, is something to celebrate.
Pauline McLeod, a children and young adult literature
specialist, says some of the best fiction sellers in the
nine- to eleven-years bracket over the past five years
include *The 91-Storey Treehouse, The War That Saved My*

Life, the *Gus* books, *Harry Potter and the Philosopher's Stone*, the Alice-Miranda series and *Grandpa's Great Escape*. Girls significantly outnumber boys at children's book clubs, and any real drop-off in reading, she says, comes in the mid to late secondary years when 'there are so many distractions and just so little time'. The platforms for reading have changed from when their older sisters were ten, with Kindles and streamed audiobooks becoming popular. 'Also, graphic novels such as the series by Raina Telgemeier have become very popular, and a lot more school libraries are stocking graphic novels,' she says.

The music our ten-agers say they are listening to is equally eclectic, with Billie Eilish, Taylor Swift, Katy Perry, Guy Sebastian, Amy Shark, Lady Gaga, Justin Bieber and Adele all ranking highly. But the role of musicals is clear, too, and the soundtracks from *Wicked*, *Matilda*, *Hamilton*, *Annie* and *Mary Poppins* play into earphones the country wide. The power of the musical is heart-warming . . . and educational. One mother told me on Facebook that her daughter had learned a lot of language through musicals, and 'not just the words but "What's a bastard?", "What's a whore?"' From *Hamilton* she also learnt about history and human rights. Another mother joined our Facebook conversation. She said she and her daughter spent hours 'diving deep into the history of the American Revolution, about slavery, about King George and his "madness", sexism, misogyny. It [*Hamilton*] is an excellent conversation starter!' These are ten-year-olds, revelling in the story of American founding father Alexander Hamilton! This should bring all of us joy; our future is in good hands.

Author Dannielle Miller says she has always been reluctant to 'throw too much shade' on what our daughters are watching, listening to and following. 'I think that's boring and predictable. And I think we have always traditionally done that. We've always rolled our eyes at the cultural icons that young people gravitate towards. So I don't know if it's necessarily helpful to try to tell them that you shouldn't be interested in this person, or that this person is boring,' she says. Instead, we need to give girls the skills to understand the context around what they are watching. 'It's about giving them that capacity to critically assess what they see that's really important.' They need to know that their online idols didn't pay for the clothes they are wearing. They were given them. They need to know that the exotic locations that sit as their backdrops are fake, or sponsored.

Although some experts disagree on the appropriateness of some of the television programs our ten-year-olds are watching, Miller's point is that they too can be used as life lessons. It's easier to have a conversation, and to influence thought, at ten than it might be at fourteen, for example, and even television programs like *The Bachelor* (which also registered with these 500 girls) could be used for that purpose. 'I think it's dangerous to try to make moral judgments about any of the celebrities or the women that they're interested in, either, because the truth is we don't really know [everything about them or their backgrounds],' she says. Her thinking around this was influenced by an exchange with her own daughter. 'I saw this magazine cover and it was aimed at young children (ten- to twelve-year-olds), and it was about how you can become an Insta entrepreneur.' It detailed how to start, what branding might be useful, how much money you could make and how to build a following. 'I was horrified and mortified, and then my daughter said to me, "Mum, it's actually really quite smart. That is the world that we are growing up in, and whether you like it or not, that is a legitimate career path."' Miller says sometimes we need to check ourselves and our preconceived notions, because we grew up at a different time from our children. 'The world has shifted and we can't roll it back,' she says.

Generally, what our girls are watching and listening to and reading is cause for celebration. Whether it is the television program on her smart device, the book on her bedside table or the music being streamed into her earphones, her choices might be broader than those of her parents. While we can applaud what our children are watching, reading and listening to, one thing raises the concern of parents and experts, and that is the power of online influencers – those on the other end of a device who can have millions of followers, exert brand power bigger than we can envisage, and who can play an enormous part in determining what a ten-year-old looks for, how she thinks and how she acts. This is the influence that needs monitoring with our ten-year-olds. It's not so much what they are consuming that raises the concern of experts here, but *how* they are consuming, and the message they take from the myriad anonymous or celebrity pop culture influencers who fill their headphones and screens.

To the issue of how, first. This generation is more connected than any previous generation; their music is in their pocket and their television is on demand. They have apps to sleep, to exercise, to learn new dances and even to learn new languages. Smart devices are part and parcel of how they live, and twenty-four-hour connectivity adds a dimension to their lives that many parents genuinely struggle to understand. There is no white space. No downtime. Less chance to think. Everything is now. Queuing or waiting means something is broken. Gratification is instant. One school wellbeing officer says that this has become such an issue that girls struggle with slow breathing exercises that are designed to create a sense of calm in stressful situations. She says that, in some cases, the need to have things immediately meant that if they could not master slow breathing in a couple of minutes, the girls thought they had failed.

Instant gratification also means struggles with anticipation. In *Being 14*, I give an example that's worth repeating here. Explain to your ten-year-old how you, at her age, captured a moment on camera.[1] They'll need to understand that a camera was not a button on a phone. First we had to adjust the focus, because that was not automatic. And then, having taken a photograph, we'd have to take another eleven or twenty-three or thirty-five photographs before 'developing' any of them. But once the roll (that will need explaining too) was full, we'd take it on a trip – by foot or bike or car – to the local pharmacy. (I love this part for the incredulous looks on their faces.) And a week later – a whole week! – we'd venture back to pick up the photographs armed with two things. First, money, for photographs were not cheap (and that meant we thought about every photo we took), and second, a delightful sense of anticipation. It's this that has been stolen from many of our children – the desire to wait for something or to work towards it – and we need to find a way to give it back to them.

The 'how' that experts express concern about envelops the access girls have to TikTok at 7 am and a friend at 9 pm, the lure of the latest friendship chat, the Fear Of Missing Out, the need to have the latest jeans, and to never not be connected. And there is no doubt this young generation, who can be as savvy as they are influential in getting what they want, is front and centre for marketers and those influencers across social media who target them. Instagram usage has grown tenfold over the past five years, and while influencers change, their power is phenomenal. Many have millions of followers. Billie Eilish has 64.7 million followers on Instagram, and a photo can prompt a million likes. Kim Kardashian is famous for being famous, thanks to a series of never-ending posts. And they all use it to sell commercial goods and influence thinking. One post, by Selena Gomez, in which she showed off a new handbag, drew 4.5 million likes. She was the most followed Instagrammer in the world in 2018, before being surpassed by footballer Cristiano Ronaldo.[2] Kylie Jenner, showing off her translucent skin, can receive 6.5 million likes. Her claim to fame? She founded cosmetic company Kylie Cosmetics and is a member of the Jenner-Kardashian clan, which includes sister Kendall Jenner and half-siblings Kim Kardashian, Kourtney Kardashian, Khloé Kardashian, Rob Kardashian, Brandon Jenner and Brody Jenner. Kendall Jenner became a model largely thanks to her Instagram success. The influencer marketing industry was set to grow to almost $10 billion in 2020. Four years earlier, in 2016, it was worth $1.7 billion. Almost 400 new 'influencer marketing-focused agencies and platforms' were set up in 2019.[3] Commercial firms are onto this – and use micro-marketing campaigns to target their customers. The most common measure of influencer marketing success is now conversions or sales.

'Who the hell are these people?' Detective Inspector Jon Rouse asks. 'They are not role models for our children.' His plea to every ten-year-old, and their parents, is this: 'Look at your digital footprint online, please, and minimise it. Don't take leadership from these influencers and think that that's a good thing.' Part of his concern is driven by the power of influencers in encouraging children to widen their online footprint. 'So they do things for people to get more followers.' He applauds the move by Instagram to not register the number of likes a user receives, because it had become 'almost like a drug for people'. School counsellor Marcelle Nader-Turner says the influence of social media is almost impossible to measure. 'It's like something in the drinking water because no-one can really identify it anymore,' she says. 'It's so pervasive and so all-encompassing in their lives that they can no longer find the edges of where their life ends and stuff begins. They no longer have the ability to be able to withstand that influence because I don't even know that they are able to identify what it is anymore.'

The power of mentors to this group is raised repeatedly, and the need for it is driven by the fact that many girls, at this age, are taking a step back from Dad and working out how much they want – or don't want – to be like Mum. It's the perfect time to expand their horizons and look to other adults who can be village guides for them. Principal Dr Toni Meath urges mentors to include 'good adults who are also comfortable in their own skin and who model authenticity'. She says 'every teacher should be like that', but this impressionable age means it could also include older siblings, an aunt or family friend who the ten-year-old looks up to and thinks is really cool. 'Importantly,' she says, 'they're not cool because of what they look like. They're cool because of how they think and what they want to do.' For a child who loves science, does she know Dr Karl Kruszelnicki? Does she know of Malala? Or Greta Thunberg? Or David Attenborough? 'It's about people being really passionate and true,' she says. 'It's not about what they look like. They're not just famous for nothing.'

The depth of sway that influencers have on our ten-agers is unfathomable. Ros Curtis, principal of a Brisbane all-girls school, makes this observation. Often children choose music that is almost 'a violent reaction' to their parents' choice. Their parents' music offends them. 'Many think it is unlistenable. "That it's not music!"' Her view is that they arrive at this feeling not because of differences in what they are listening to compared with their parents, but *how* they are doing it – the context around it. 'I think when I was growing up there would have been things that influenced me that my parents wouldn't have had much to do with. But it was contained. It was nowhere near as widespread and as broad. There's no parent who can keep a handle on it now, no teacher who can keep a handle on it.' Brisbane's John Paul College principal Karen Spiller says she believes we don't actually understand how significant these influencers are in a girl's life. 'The best way to keep these in check is to make sure that kids have their phones, laptops, iPads and other devices monitored as they should – parental checks, take them at night – all those things. And then you've just got to be having conversations with the kids.'

A big driver in pop culture choices comes down to a child's journey to self-identity. Who do they want to be? What do they like about this person or that person? Marcelle Nader-Turner says the journey is littered with questions. 'What does who she is mean? Does that mean who she is? Or who she thinks she's supposed to be? ... I don't think we can say, with the kind of impact and influence that social media has, that a young person would have any idea about who she is, in the way we might have,' she says. Brisbane school principal Catherine O'Kane says it's a hard track for girls. 'I never had to compare myself to this picture of this glamour person, who's also ten. And if I could teach the girls one thing it would be to not compare themselves.' To make her point, she uses Ted Roosevelt's assertion that 'comparison is the thief of joy'. 'It is so true, because if that is what you do on Instagram, if all you do is look at others and judge yourself by what you see, you will be extremely unhappy, I can guarantee that. But that's what they're doing.'

Finding themselves takes time. Many parents might remember struggling with that, too, but without any online pressure. For me, the urge to define myself arrived some time between the ages of ten and eleven and saw me enter the local council building in my hometown of Dalby, three hours west of Brisbane, with the intention of changing my name. Looking back, the woman answering my query must have thought, from those seven words – 'Hello, I want to change my name' – that this exchange would make her week. She called over her colleagues, almost gleefully, and they huddled across the counter to discuss the plan that would change my life. It wasn't that I disliked the name, and there were three 'Madonnas' in my class (a nod to Queensland country Catholicism), but it set me up for failure in class, where every admonishment ended with 'and to think you were given the name Madonna . . .' In my class there was also a girl called Patricia, who had perfectly straight and shiny hair. That appealed. Handing me a form, the council staffer asked me what name I had chosen. 'Patricia,' I said. The woman nodded. 'You need to fill out this form that goes through your current details – name, address, all those details – and bring it back to me.' I could feel success. 'Oh, and you can't change your first name without your last name,' she quipped. 'Have you thought of that?' Someone more worldly might have realised I was the butt of a Friday office joke, but my response was fast. I looked around the room. A fake and dusty old plant in the corner caught my eye. 'Plant,' I said. 'Patricia Plant.' Twenty minutes later I was back at the desk and ready to assume my new identity. The lady read my answers out loud, to the approval of her co-workers, who enjoyed the punchline so much more than I did. 'This is all good,' she announced, 'but you just need to take the form home and get your parents to sign it ... unless you are over eighteen years of age?'

All ten-year-old girls are on that journey to finding out who they are and who they want to be – a journey of self-discovery that starts before the signs of puberty are visible and travels through adolescence into adulthood. The starting and finishing line will be different for everyone, but the online world produces more forks in the road than we could ever have imagined. Of course, as pointed out elsewhere, this is not a homogenous group, and various levels of maturity and development create wide differences amongst ten-agers. Let's take the issue of allyship within the Black Lives Matter movement as one example. At fourteen and fifteen, girls can explain and embody allyship well, but at ten some struggled to articulate how they felt and what it meant to them. The ante is really amped up for our ten-agers. They are all just looking for validation and their place in an increasingly complex society.

A note here on the apparent need, at ten, for children to decide their sexuality. They hear it in music, see it on screen, and many talk about it at lunch. Ros Curtis, like many of her peer educators, expresses concern about movements that are developing in some middle schools, particularly in the US. 'It's right that kids are thinking about things,' she says. 'But it's a really difficult one to navigate, for many and varied reasons. My major thing is I want everybody to have a voice and I really want to celebrate diversity and tolerance. But I don't want to influence. And that's the tough thing.' Three other principals, in two different states, raise the same issue. 'I don't think most parents would know half of the influence these girls are under from marginal groups in society, because the cheapest way to get to people is through social media,' one says. This principal says even young mothers – who might be in their early thirties – are more likely to be hooked on Facebook or Instagram than to be on TikTok and YouTube, where girls are being influenced. A second principal is exasperated by the fact that children are not simply left to be children. 'There's plenty of time for those decisions!' she says. That principal says the voices of older students exert as much of an influence on young students as popular culture, and parents need to have open and honest conversations with their children around sexuality and what they are seeing and hearing. Another raised the issue independently.

If the matter of how children are exploring pop culture raises a first alert, their ability to distil messages comes in a close second. Taking researcher Mark McCrindle's point that ten-agers are now older younger, many of them are able to understand nuances and references that might have been lost on their parents at the same age. 'They're not ready to be there, and nor should they,' Lisa Miller says. 'I think back to the songs we used to listen to and they're no less provocative, and some of them were worse. But if we heard things that were a little bit inappropriate, we didn't really know what it meant anyway.' A nine- or ten- or eleven-year-old listens and takes in what they are ready to understand. 'I think that they have more of an awareness and understanding, through exposure, and they're able to listen to that and understand what that means.' This is the crux of this concern.

What is the take-out for girls in what they are seeing and hearing? And how do they process that? Catherine O'Kane says it's about teaching girls to be 'critical consumers'. 'So that at least if you're going to consume that message, know where it's come from and what's underneath it,' she says. They needed to understand the manipulation that might be going on, like product placement for example. 'How do you do that at ten? To me, it's about education. It's about actually naming [the manipulation], and explicitly teaching it here at school. They've got to be able to do it through critical literacy,' O'Kane says.

Too often, experts say, the take-out is that she – our ten-year-old – is not good enough. Not pretty enough.

Not clever enough. Not talented enough. Simply not enough. The amount of content at children's disposal adds to that confusion. Just consider the 'best friend concept' expounded in so much of what our girls watch on screen. Often there's a main character and a sidekick. That works well in story-telling, but not so well in the playground. How does a ten-year-old learn to differentiate? They are starting to unpack and decode messages on a whole lot of issues. But that leads to confusion, too. Are they a child? Or an adult? And what do we expect of them?

For some, those messages drive a belief that they need to be older and more sophisticated. In other cases, girls believe it's time to be interested in boys. And some of them are. At one school, I asked a small group of ten-year-old girls to write on a piece of paper what they most wanted me to explore in this research. 'Boys,' one said. 'How do you know if you like a boy?' And a second girl: 'Is it normal to like a boy when you are my age?' Those two had smartphones. Three others asked how to best pressure their parents into giving them a smartphone.

School counsellor Marcelle Nader-Turner warned that parents have a decade of parenting ahead of their child's tenth birthday and therefore need to consider how they decode the messages that wallpaper their children's lives. Children will be asking: Do I need to do what others are doing? Is being sexy important? Does it matter if I take a nude selfie of myself? 'So this is the moment where those kinds of seeds of your parenting start to bear fruit. Does your ten-year-old go, "I'm not doing that. I value myself way more than that." Because that comes from the kind of parenting that has happened. Then you've got the ten-year-old who desperately needs to feel validated and accepted by her peer group because she doesn't have a sense of that already within herself.' Girls who valued themselves, she says, were far less likely to send naked pictures of themselves, too.

From the moment children are born, parents seek support in networks – mothers' groups, or reading groups. And then, when their children start school, that continues. Parents talk at the school gate about lunch boxes and tying shoelaces. They ask each other for advice and swap tales. But once children are slightly more independent – walking to school by themselves, or catching the bus or being dispatched in a drop-off zone – that parent-to-parent contact often eases off. And that's when, every expert suggests, it needs to be turned up. What our ten-year-olds are reading and listening to and watching is a cause for celebration. The challenge sits with how they are watching it, and what message they're receiving.

Good night, sleep tight

'We can see very clearly when students aren't getting the right amount of sleep. It impacts on their health, their mental capacity, their mindset.'

Principal Susan Dalton

Emily, Kailin, Jessica and Bella are all ten, and they're explaining their sleep patterns. 'I go to bed at 7:30 pm because my parents want me to get a good sleep,' Emily says. But she's the exception. 'I have to go at 8:30 pm and lights out at 9 pm, but then I just stare at the ceiling for hours,' Kailin says. And for a ten-year-old, fifteen minutes can seem like hours. 'I don't have a bedtime,' says Jessica. 'Mum says it's part of my independence; I decide when I'm tired, which I like.' And Bella? 'I have different bedtimes depending on the day of the week. If I have school, it's

9:30 pm. On the weekend, it's whatever, unless there's a big sport game!'

That's the girls. Put the same question to parents and the answers are similarly varied:

'8:30 pm school nights; during COVID it was 10 pm.'

'Compared to her siblings at the same age, late! She used to fall asleep as soon as she went to bed, but now that she is maturing she can't get to sleep at night so we've been lenient and her bedtime is 9 pm.'

'Too late. She's a night owl. She will happily stay up until 11 pm. We try and have her asleep by 9:30 pm on school nights.'

'She doesn't have a set bedtime. Perhaps I'm a bit lenient but she's always asleep by midnight.'

When you analyse why such a variance in bedtimes exists, it comes down to four factors: those with older siblings seem to have later bedtimes; parents wanting to give their children independence often choose to do it by allowing them to decide when to head for bed; during COVID, bedtimes stretched out in some cases by two hours; and finally, bedtimes vary widely between weekdays, weekends and holidays.

Experts say almost all those factors should carry a warning. We can't choose our children's friends, even if we try to. We can't make them play a sport they hate. We can't get them to do their homework as soon as they arrive home each afternoon. There is so much, at this age, that we can't or shouldn't control – domains we need to step back from in order to help our daughters make their own good choices. But sleep is *not* one of those. Experts say this is where we can still wield powerful influence, by setting rules, encouraging its importance, being consistent and practising good 'sleep hygiene'.

Lisa Miller, the head of Strathcona Girls Grammar junior school, says teachers can spot the tired children. Their faces betray them first, she says. 'They're pale; they look tired. And then they can't cope. They're exhausted and the more that goes on, their ability to cope becomes less – and can escalate into other behaviour.' She is supported by several sleep experts who say 'sleepiness' might not always be a symptom of a lack of sleep – but a child's behaviour will be. Parents and schools need to work together here, and the fact that sleep hygiene classes are now routinely being provided to twelve- and thirteen-year-olds suggests they're not always in sync. Indeed, COVID has provided an added challenge here. Schools were sending laptops home for children as young as ten, and even younger in some cases, to facilitate online learning. Alert to the dangers, some schools restricted their students' access so they could not be on them late into the night. For example, one all-girls school invested in a program that shut the device down at 6 pm. 'We were responsible, because we were sending the school device home,' one teacher says. The school was taking away the family's decision-making power by providing the computer, so it felt it had a responsibility to ensure the device was used properly. But that did not sit well with all parents, says the same teacher. Some believed that if a device was provided, students should have been able to access it at any time. In this case, though, the school was unapologetic. 'I think parents also need to make some of those hard choices for their children,' the teacher says.

Educators are unanimous in believing that sleep is a health policy issue that needs stronger attention. Teachers say they see the consequences of it in Maths and English, on the sports field and in trumpet ensemble. Ten-year-old girls, exhausted, push back against early bedtimes for several reasons: their body clock, with the onset of puberty, has changed and they struggle to fall asleep as they might have done a year earlier; they want to stay up later to prove they are growing up; their heads are still buzzing with the latest TikTok or online friendship drama; or anxiety is filling the darkness each time they close their eyes. But it's how tiredness manifests itself twelve hours later that should have us all reconsidering our home sleep policy. Kym Amor is the foundation principal at Foxwell State Secondary College at Coomera, on the Gold Coast, and she says schools are constantly reminding parents of its importance. As a former primary school leader, she says she would routinely send home research papers – 'so parents wouldn't think we were telling them how to parent' – reminding them that they were 'in control of when their child goes to sleep – at least until their teenage years'. In other schools, students are being taught how to sleep, and individual families are being targeted, in many instances, with a plea for a child to bed down earlier. 'We do the general talk, but now we're talking to individual families because their child is personally affected,' one school principal says.

Screen time is certainly a factor, says Gold Coast principal Susan Dalton. 'And I think that that's where parents struggle,' she says. Sometimes it's easier to 'let it go than fight it'. Most parents can understand that – but her plea is that we prioritise the health, mental capacity and mindset that a good night's sleep can provide. Those with poor sleep patterns presented each morning moodier than their peers, and routinely did not ask as many questions in class. 'We really push the three Rs here – roles, relationships and routine – and the routine is critical,' says Dalton. 'Research shows us that if you can have a solid routine, your capacity to work and learn the next day is much greater; you just feel more confident – and curious – to ask questions.'

This is not an issue exclusive to ten-year-old girls. Four in every ten Australians are not getting sufficient sleep, and the direct financial cost of this sleep deficit is $26.2 billion each year. 'If health and wellbeing costs are considered, the cost rises to $66.3 billion annually.' These are the findings of a 2019 report on sleep health awareness in Australia, titled 'Bedtime Reading'. Even more worryingly, the report says that between 2016 and 2017, 3017 deaths in Australia could be attributed to inadequate sleep.

The Royal Australasian College of Physicians told an Australian parliamentary inquiry that 70 per cent of South Australian teens were getting insufficient sleep every school night. The Adelaide Institute for Sleep Health drew on Canadian research in its submission to the same inquiry, saying 85 per cent of teens did not get enough sleep. Wellbeing in Schools Australia warned that children feared disconnection from their online friends and were running electronic devices twenty-four hours a day. 'The result being,' said the submission, 'they are reporting to teachers of having their sleep regularly interrupted during the night.' Similarly, the Sleep Health Foundation found children who had three hours of screen time each day were more likely to have higher rates of poor sleep – 'and poorer educational outcomes than children who spend less time in front of screens'. It also linked poor sleep and mental health by providing the example that 'poor sleep in young, non-depressed Australian women was found to increase the risk of subsequent depression more than four-fold within a decade'. That alone should provide cause for us to revisit our children's – and perhaps our own – sleep patterns. But the Australasian Sleep Association went further, saying that inadequate sleep affects the functioning of every cell in the body.[1]

So is there any science behind how much sleep a ten-year-old needs? How much does it vary between children? Is it the amount of sleep or the quality that matters? And how instrumental is an early bedtime in that? 'Great questions,' says Professor Tim Olds from the School of Health Sciences at the University of South Australia. The answers, he says, are complex. 'The recommendation is nine to eleven hours of sleep duration for a ten-year-old. That's based on a consensus view of a whole lot of paediatricians.' Professor Olds conducted a study to measure sleep with wrist-worn devices on participants, who all also kept sleep diaries. Researchers then considered a stack of gold-standard measures – from language ability to fitness levels, blood fats, academic performance and bone strength. This 2016 study was part of the Longitudinal Study of Australian Children, and included 1000 children aged eleven. Activity patterns and outcomes were monitored to consider the best mix of activities or the optimum way to spend twenty-four hours.

'When we looked at language development we found the kids who did best on that had very little sleep – less than eight hours,' Professor Olds says. This could be a consequence of staying up late and studying, or waking early to complete school work. 'But at the other end of the scale, the kids who did best on mental health had more than eleven hours' sleep. The other outcomes were in the middle.' Surprisingly, those attributes that were associated with less sleep were better academic performance, cognition, language and fitness – both running and jumping. However, the children who slept more were thinner, confirming other studies in that area (it's not the same for adults). 'The general point is that the ideal amount of sleep, as part of activity composition, will vary according to the outcome. And nine to eleven hours' sleep has turned out to be not a bad outcome. Most of them are within that nine- to eleven-hour band,' Professor Olds says. But some children only managed eight hours during the week – nowhere near sufficient for most good outcomes relating to blood fats, bone strength and respiratory health – and the shortest nightly sleep recorded was six hours.

A consequence of the need to get adequate rest time is that other activities are sacrificed to allow those extra hours of sleep. 'If you sleep one more hour, you've got to do one hour less of something else . . . The time has to come from somewhere, and where it comes from is important,' Professor Olds says. It becomes a trade-off – what's important to an individual child and their family? A longer sleep and stronger mental health might be the aim of one family, but at the other end of the spectrum a shorter sleep and a better academic report card might be celebrated by another family. Of course, this simplifies all those other factors like blood, bone and respiratory health.

Just as important as how much sleep a child gets is the timing of sleep. 'All our studies show that early to bed, early to rise is so much better,' Professor Olds says. 'If you have two kids and they both have ten hours' sleep, but one goes to bed early and one goes to bed late, the kid who goes to bed early does better on almost every measure you can imagine.' So what does 'early' mean, for a ten-year-old? 'What's early is largely dependent on the school day. On school days almost every child in the country gets up somewhere between 7 am and 7:30 am. They need to be fed and clothed and out the door. So if you want nine hours' sleep, they have to be in bed by 10 pm – that's the latest they could go. If they want eleven hours' sleep they'd have to be in bed by 8 pm. Being in bed by 9 pm is a reasonable estimate to get that sleep.' But that's only if they nod off quickly. Many girls differentiate between bedtimes and *sleep* times. 'I go to bed at 8:15 and I am normally asleep by 9:15,' one says. 'It's supposed to be 8:30 pm but by the time I read and do other stuff it's much later,' another says. 'I go to bed at 9:30 pm but that's not when I go to sleep,' says a third.

Professor Olds, who goes to bed at 8 pm each night and rises very early, says the third factor in sleep – in addition to amount and timing – is variability. This is crucial, given the responses by parents who allow their children to go to bed at different times on school nights, at the weekend and during holidays. 'The kids who have a more regular pattern – that's including weekends and weekdays – do better, other things being equal,' he says. So if 9 pm is the stipulated bedtime, it should remain 9 pm on weekend nights and during the holidays. The rationale for this is not obvious but is borne out in the research. 'I suspect part of the importance is that kids who are consistent tend to have that "early-to-bed, early-to-rise" pattern,' he says. Additionally, children staying up late are likely to be playing games or watching television, or even snacking. Children who rise early are more likely to be having an early, healthy breakfast, and perhaps even exercise. That better 'fit' with ideal dietary and physical activity patterns might be one reason why consistent early rising is beneficial; another is the possibility that they are more in sync with their biorhythms.

The quality of sleep is important, too, despite an inability by researchers to measure it effectively. In the absence of recognised measures, researchers have looked at sleep efficiency, or the amount of time spent asleep, rather than lying in bed. 'We know, for example, that for memory consolidation it's important to have certain types of sleep – slow-wave sleep, which is that first, really deep sleep, and the REM sleep, which is the last sleep before you wake up,' Professor Olds says. 'They're important for different types of memory – one for memory of facts and the other for memory of how to do things.'

So that's some of the science. But how does all this play out tonight, in the homes of ten- and eleven-year-olds in Geelong and Hobart, Townsville and Adelaide? 'The trick is to get kids into the mood for sleep at the time they're really sleepy,' Professor Olds says. 'We have these waves of sleep washing over us every ninety minutes or so. The first thing is that when that wave of sleep hits, kids have got to be changed, they've got to be in their pyjamas, they've got to have done something quiet, they've got to be ready to go to bed. That's why regularity is really important.'

It's also the basis of sleep hygiene, which is a life skill increasingly being taught in schools. In my home, we changed how sleep was considered after hearing the evidence put to me by experts while researching *Being 14*. Sleep needs to be planned, just like school lunch boxes. It's tricky and fiddly because each child is different. But a warm cup of milk, a bath, no screens for forty-five minutes before bed, a dark room and a hug has worked wonders in my household, for three years now. And while the recipe for each child is different, the impact of good sleep hygiene is enormous. Senior principal research fellow in the Department of Paediatrics at Monash University, Professor Rosemary Horne, says it's important to get sleep right early, because by the time a child is thirteen there might be less parental control or supervision around bedtimes. 'The main thing is to have a set routine, no matter what age. Dinner, do your homework, maybe a bit of television, have your shower, read your book, maybe a drink of milk and then calm time in bed. And try to do that at a similar time every night,' she says.

Professor Horne also raises the issue of how extracurricular activities can interrupt routines. The number of activities and opportunities now on offer to ten-year-olds is tremendous. When I was ten and living in a small Queensland country town, the choices were limited. Speech and Drama was my lifeline, but lessons were short. A big family meant sporting fees needed to be budgeted, so it was Little Athletics on a Friday night, to let off a week of steam, and tennis each Saturday afternoon. But when we compare our after-school activities with those of our daughters, it is a different world. Public and private schools and independent and community organisations offer dozens of sports, along with an array of other opportunities, from theatre sports to United Nations debates, early rowing training to Maths Olympiads. Those activities are splendid, but they can also sap hours out of a day and need to be considered as part of girls' daily activity make-up. The best piece of advice received for my own daughters, when each of them turned ten and moved to middle school, was that they would want to try everything – but should be limited to two activities.

We added the rule that once they started something, they needed to stick with it for the semester or season, whether it turned out to be an activity they liked or didn't like. Professor Olds agrees that the take-up of activities – and sometimes the push by parents for ten-year-olds to star in Mandarin and violin and a host of other activities – can play a role in creating time-deficit problems. 'A lot of kids just want their time to play, so when they're in the room by themselves they've got their time to play. I think that's driving it a lot. I think if we gave them a bit more free time and let them regulate their time, we might not have all these problems,' he says.

The effect of screens on a child's brain, ahead of bedtime, is regularly discussed. Professor Horne says much evidence exists to show it 'disrupts you going to sleep and disrupts your sleep patterns'. Screens include televisions, laptops, tablets and phones. 'The old way we did it – where you went to bed and read books and then went to sleep – is much better.' She admits that digital ubiquity makes that easier said than done. 'I know from my own children. The oldest one didn't get a phone until Year 12, and then her sister, who was six years younger, got it when she started Year 7. There's been this whole change, and a lot of schools bring in laptops in Years 4 and 5.'

Sarah Blunden is a professor of psychology and head of paediatric sleep research at Central Queensland

University's Adelaide Campus. She is also the Sleep Health Foundation's paediatric spokesperson. She notes the 'massive' link between sleep and memory. 'We know that during sleep we consolidate memory. We know that because researchers have done many studies where you put somebody to sleep. You give them a learning task beforehand – for example, a list of numbers or letters – and you deprive them of sleep duration, or you disrupt their sleep, or fragment it, or you deprive them of REM sleep, and all of those will make those who've had that disrupted sleep less able to remember those things.' It's a tried and true experiment, she says.

Sleep needs are different between children as they grow and develop. 'Sleep patterns change with puberty and they become very different from what they were prior to puberty,' Professor Blunden says. Our individual circadian clocks – informed by light, temperature, rhythm and melatonin – alert us to when our bodies want to go to sleep. In adolescence, melatonin secretion is delayed. It starts kicking in later in the evening. Whereas a prepubescent child might be sleepy at 9 pm, at puberty 80 per cent of pubescent adolescents will want to go to sleep later. This can be exacerbated by parents allowing children to choose their own bedtime. 'Personally, and through my private practice and research, I believe that at ten, even though they might be physically mature, they are not cognitively mature,' Professor Blunden says. 'They are still a ten-year-old and they don't have the emotional and cognitive capacity to understand what an eighteen-year-old can.' And the more parents helped children have a 'predictable and regular and not variable bedtime', the better they were in every possible way.

Those three factors – predictability, regularity and consistency – are raised repeatedly by all experts, along with that recommended guide of between nine and eleven hours' sleep each night. But how do you know if your child needs nine hours or eleven hours? 'Every child is different in how much sleep they need,' Professor Blunden says. 'Between nine and eleven hours is a very different thing. Child One might need nine hours; Child Two needs eleven. That's a big difference. So how do we know what's good for them? The only way is through observation and seeing how they are going.' Inevitably that can lead to friction between parents and children. Indeed, most of the children Professor Blunden is seeing in private practice now are 'so stressed' that they can't sleep. 'They try to go to sleep. Their parents are saying, "They're not sleeping", so the message to that child very clearly is that they're doing the wrong thing. They're not sleeping; they're disrupting the family. It's becoming a big family stress.' The increase in numbers in her waiting room is largely attributable to primary and middle-school children. 'Adolescents have always been a problem, preschoolers have always been a problem, but I'm seeing a rise in middle-school [kids with sleep difficulties],' Professor Blunden says.

So if she had an open chequebook and was made Minister for Sleep, what would she do? 'I would educate every child – not just ten-year-olds – to understand sleep as one of the three pillars of health, like diet and exercise. It should be the third pillar. Sleep is the foundation of all that stuff. Understanding that trifecta is really important.' And she'd reduce our competitive culture. 'We're too busy achieving. We're too busy being top of the class. Not everyone's like that, but there's a very competitive culture. And that's not something a chequebook would change, but I'd dearly love to give people back the control and make them understand that if you control your sleep, you can control a lot of other stuff.' Even at the age of ten.

Parenting ten-agers

'Get them out, be involved with them, form
those really strong relationships with them,
take them camping, do things with them
because it'll be time well spent, not only for
your relationship with them as a parent, but
for them as a developing young woman.'

Dr Toni Meath, principal, Melbourne Girls Grammar

When the coronavirus began to close the curtain on some school productions, many were staged early, but with restrictions. In some, no audience was allowed, but school staff advised parents that they would record it and make it available online. That's what one school did. 'And I find it quite extraordinary that parents went against my wishes,' one school leader says, 'and broke in at night, and sat there to watch their daughter perform.' When confronted, parents said they needed to do it for their daughters. 'They said their daughters would have been anxious and depressed and that it could have put their health at risk if they weren't there.'

This type of parental involvement is not unusual, and school leaders and teachers amass examples of parents who hover, or helicopter, over their children, wanting to protect them at any cost. Writing letters of complaint when their child is not made class captain. Providing outside references for a child to star in a school play. Arguing with a Maths teacher over a single percentage mark on a test. 'We don't have a problem with kids,' a senior educator says. 'We have a problem with this generation of parents.' It's a harsh judgement, but other experts raised this too. 'As parents,' says one, 'we are obsessed with our kids having an amazing magical childhood and school experience.' One school leader says, 'Parents want their child to have the best day every day, and life doesn't work like that.' And from another: 'I worry about these girls' grounded-ness. I worry that [our girls] are growing up in a world of entitlement and losing sight of reality.' Of the kids these parents raise, another principal says: 'They're wrapped in cotton wool. Parents need to know it's okay for them to fall over and hurt themselves. It's okay to climb that tree and even have the experience of a broken arm.' And another school leader: 'I think we have a massive obliga-tion to get them to open their eyes to the rest of the world and live beyond their own bubble.' A male Year 5 teacher doesn't mince words: 'Little princesses are being rescued by their parents all the time. I find it extraordinary the number of parents who have to go in to bat for their children and don't understand that they need to take a step back and let that child work it out themselves.' 'The level of protectiveness' in some instances, says a Sydney principal, is 'quite shocking'. And growing.

Like many experienced educators, Helen Adams, from Perth, has over many years of teaching seen how parenting has changed. It is all too apparent today that many parents do not want their child to suffer setbacks or disappointments. 'Some want them wrapped in cotton wool,' she says. Her plea is that children, at this age, be given the space to develop independence. Another principal, in an affluent area that rode the last economic boom, says parents want their daughters' journeys to be ideal, without any potholes. 'They want everything for them to be perfect. They'll buy them designer clothes, for example. And I worry about the sort of flow-on effect – that their whole life has to be perfect.' This principal gives the example of dance. Once upon a time, girls might have learnt tap or ballet or Irish dancing. But now many girls do several types, several times a week. 'These girls have been bred to believe that this is the norm; that you do everything, and you are entitled to be able to do whatever you want, whenever you want.'

One study of 1000 US adults showed that more than four in five, as children, had regular chores, compared with less than 30 per cent of their own children.[1] Kate Julian, in her article 'What Happened to American Childhood?', says chores provided children with two things: an ability to tolerate discomfort, and a sense of personal competence. 'This may be why doing chores from age three or four onward has been found to be a very strong predictor of academic, professional and relational success in young adulthood,' she says. Her investigation also raised the view that modern upper-middle-class parents were perceived 'not as flailing but as the opposite: too hyper, too competent, too vigilant'. 'Despite more than a decade's evidence that helicopter parenting is counterproductive, kids today are perhaps more overprotected, more leery of adulthood, more in need of therapy [than they ever have been].' Julian's investigation asked whether children's mental health was related less to 'our hard-driving style than to our exhaustion and guilt and failure to put our foot down'. While many parents complain about children being 'thin-skinned and susceptible to peer pressure', maybe we are the ones who are 'hypersensitive to the judgement of our peers and, especially, of our children. And the harder we try to do the right thing – the more we nurture them, the more quickly we respond to their needs – the more we tie ourselves in knots.'[2]

Daisy Turnbull, author of *50 Risks to Take With Your Kids*, is the director of wellbeing at Sydney's St Catherine's School, and she says that as a teacher she has previously had parents call her to ask for their child to get out of detention. The rationales vary but can include that the student is sorry, is busy, or wasn't responsible for any wrongdoing. Turnbull's personal favourite, though, was the rationale that it was the parent's fault! 'And I teach teenagers,' she writes. 'If the parent is stepping in to defend their child at age fifteen or seventeen, you can bet they were doing it beforehand, too.' It's between the ages of six and twelve that children develop the skill of competence, she says, and that's when parents need to step back and let their child do things and get better at things. 'This is where you become a coach rather than the boss, and recognise your child's own ability to develop and grow,' she says. Coaching allows children to make more decisions, and to take responsibility for them. If parents do not practise this, a child's ability, confidence and self-esteem – all key ingredients as they move to high school – could be hurt. Says Turnbull: 'As a high school teacher, I have seen many cohorts of students leave Year 12, and the observation I've made is that the students who thrive, who are leaders, who excel at sport or music or debating, or who are just really kind humans, are those with parents who have developed their own child's competence, and done so steadily, since they were young.' It was something that was built over years, with constant attention. 'The more you do it, the more it will become part of your everyday parenting.'

Being authoritarian is not the answer to promoting autonomy in kids. The more authoritarian we are, the less likely they are to respond and develop their own sense of responsibility. It's how we parent that's important. Gradually, as our daughters move towards being tweens, we need to get them to take responsibility for themselves. It might be doing chores, within a set timeframe, or making the decision themselves over a birthday present for a friend, or choosing their own outfit to wear. 'When you can give them that option rather than tell them what to do, and give them more choice, then they'll be more respectful and also take more responsibility and think more about the decisions they make,' Turnbull says.

Allow a child to grow up, without hovering, without being there ready to catch them: this is the advice recommended by teachers to parents – irrespective of the make-up of the family unit. A ten-ager might be living with her biological parents, or with one of them and a step-parent. She might live between parents or with a single parent. Her grandparents might be her carers, or her aunt and uncle, or foster carers, or a dozen other configurations. Who she lives with doesn't matter as much as the lessons she receives from those who cherish her. Paul Dillon, who spends his days with older children warning about drugs and alcohol, says role-modelling is a huge factor. 'Your child is picking up evidence at between three and eight,' he says. He gives examples of studies, relating to alcohol, that show children as young as three can have beverage-specific knowledge, from the age of four they start to know about alcoholic content of beverages, and from age six they start to know about adult drinking norms, like who is drinking and in what circumstances.[3] They've seen it. They've learnt it.

Matt Sanders, a professor of clinical psychology and founder of the Triple P Positive Parenting Program, which is now used in more than twenty-five countries and has been translated into twenty-one languages, says it is the environment, not the family make-up, that is crucial to good parenting. Children, when young, need to feel safe and cared for. But taking up the point about being over-protective, he sees 'anxious, hovering parents who are so fretful about their children's safety that they prevent them from climbing a slide, climbing a tree or doing things that involves elements of risk'. Doing that risks children becoming avoidant and anxious, he says. An encouraging environment, where positive feedback is provided, allows them to learn to be civil and pleasant and polite. And they need boundaries and limits and rules. 'There's some parents who think, "Oh, you can't have these over-programmed, overly-prescribed circumstances with kids, because that's highly controlling." But there's another way to look at this – and that is that kids learn to cooperate with reasonable, age-appropriate rules and instructions.' That's a life skill, because if children don't learn to cooperate and get on with others, they end up 'ruling the roost' and home is dominated by children imposing their wishes. In that case, Professor Sanders warns, 'you'll have kids who become incredibly self-centred. It will be "me me me, now now now",' he says.

Many parents, in this research, eschewed structures and parent-dictated rules, suggesting they were outdated and limited their children, preventing them from learning and making their own decisions. But it's not just Professor Sanders who puts the case for structures and rules; amongst educators, counsellors and psychologists, it was almost unanimous. School principal Ros Curtis adds another argument against a no-limits parenting policy, saying it allows a ten-year-old to 'blame her parents' and escape involvement in activities. 'She can say, "I'd love to be able to do it, but my mother will find out and this will happen to me."' Keep up with the structures and keep up with the talks about values, she says. Like others, Curtis recommends scenario-playing with ten-year-olds. What would you do if someone was following you? What would you do if a boy suggested this? What would you do if your friend asked you do that? Making it real through scenarios allows a ten-year-old to determine how she would react in different situations. 'Unless they think about it before they're in that situation, they've got no chance,' Curtis says.

What children don't get from their parents they'll look for elsewhere, says psychologist Karen Young. 'So they need that sense of belonging and acceptance. They need that sense of power and influence, because if they don't get that, if they don't have a sense of their own power and their own strength, they will look to other people to lead them.' Her point is that before our ten-year-olds gravitate towards their peers, the foundations need to be set – and strongly – so that they come back to us for guidance. They know we are not going to shame them. And Young urges that we not judge them. 'We might not like everything they do, and sometimes we will put heavy limits on what they do, but it's not done through shame,' she says. 'The mistake I see is a lot of parents coming in when kids are fourteen, fifteen and sixteen to try and have that influence. By then, it's going to be a lot harder.' She says if children are talking about an episode at school, our reaction is important. If we flare up or shut the discussion down, next time they might not open up. It doesn't mean agreeing with them, though. 'It means I won't judge you,' explains Young. 'Come to me with anything, [because] I can handle anything you say. And of course, sometimes you know they'll say things and we'll just sort of explode, but we can't do it in front of them.' Giving them time is important, too. 'If we don't, the conversations that we want them to have when they're older, they're not going to come to us. So we're teaching them, when they're young, the type of relationship they can have with us when they're older.' This addressed a concern many mothers expressed during this project: how to have their daughters continue to confide in them once solid friendships took hold. 'How can I create time rituals to stay close to my daughters as they grow? After losing my mother at about this age, I struggle with what role I play in this changing time,' one mother said. And another: 'I've heard that girls can shut their mums out and treat them like the enemy as they get nearer to their teens. How can I make sure this doesn't happen to us?' Time, and hugs, as you will read later, can work miracles.

School counsellor Marcelle Nader-Turner says the girls who do better are those with good emotional literacy. 'They know what feelings feel like – where they sit in the body and what they are called; they know how to talk about feelings; they have had their feelings validated by someone, so they know that their feelings are real,' she says. 'They know that someone in their home will acknowledge the emotions they are experiencing, and that home is a place where emotions and feelings are discussed.' Without doubt, the most common difficulties arise in homes where emotions and feelings are never discussed. '[Girls] don't know where to begin with identifying or explaining what's happening to them,' Nader-Turner says, 'and they don't know how to find ways to calm themselves in their distress. They are more likely to experience anxiety, depression and self-harm.'

When mothers are asked to describe the bond they have with their ten-year-old, the answers could fill a football stadium. But common themes pop up: the difficulty in parenting; how hard it is when a ten-year-old starts to pull away, or stops talking, or wants more privacy; the influence of our own mothers and fathers on the way we parent. The power of a father's role came through strongly, too. 'We can underestimate the power of positive influence, of having an awesome, warm, happy father in our daughters' lives,' one woman says. She continues: 'My sister and I had a great relationship with our father, and still do. My husband is pro-women and has employed all females in senior roles in his business. And his mother is also a strong personality like me – as are his sisters. I'm sad that this generation of kids never got to have the freedom – experiences both good and bad – of being let loose and growing up with other kids roaming the streets and parks like we did in the 1980s. This generation is so scheduled, organised, online. It's a different world, as much as I try to balance it out for them.'

So how do mothers judge the bond they have with their tween daughters?

'Definitely better than my mother and me at the same age!'

'I feel like I have a very open relationship with my daughter. We spend fifteen to twenty minutes at bedtime talking about her day and my day, and if there's anything troubling her.'

'She is beginning to need more privacy, especially when talking with her friends, but if she has questions she comes to me.'

'We are very close. I enjoy her immensely. And am disappointed that she is starting to care more about what her friends think than what I think.'

'We are close 90 per cent of the time. She tells me most things. I won't say she tells me everything because I don't know if that's true.'

'Not as strong as I would like. She has started to want more privacy and independence so I'm trying to find a balance of what works for us both. She can be very vocal about her unhappiness with how I parent!'

'I'm close to all my children but my ten-year-old doesn't tend to tell me everything like my older daughter does.'

'My ten-year-old can be sneaky and this is a struggle for us.'

'Very open. She has been told she can ask me anything and that nothing is off limits. She has been told that *for me to answer a question that may concern me, she needs to tell me how she heard/where she heard it. For example, I gave her the sex talk and told her she could ask me anything. The next day she asked me what anal sex was! Good grief! I asked and she told me she heard it on* Law and Order!'

'*I feel like she can tell me anything but I also know from personal experience that my mum would have said the same thing.*'

'*She is my best friend.*'

That last answer irks Karen Spiller, principal of John Paul College in Brisbane. 'I would urge parents not to be their child's friend . . . She's your daughter and she's lovely – but she's not your best friend.' Spiller says it's understandable that parents want to make everything smooth for their daughters, but if they see them as friends and don't let them experience hardship, they will never experience challenge – and that is important for their development.

Professor Matt Sanders says a big concern for parents of tween girls is the pressure applied upon them by their daughters. It might be for a new phone, or the right clothes, or a change in rules. 'Often they're not cognitively and developmentally mature enough to realise that what they're requesting is not appropriate,' he says. Unsurprisingly, technology created the other challenge to parenting. 'Social media is playing an increasing role, particularly once kids get their own phones. They want to be part of that peer network. But at the same time, there's a dominance of screen time anyway. Within many families it's a real battleground. And it's a battleground because it's hard. It's hard for parents to constantly be placing boundaries and limits around kids when they're testing them all the time. So then you get family conflict that [escalates] to a level that is sometimes very hard to eliminate completely. You go on a camping trip where there's no mobile reception and you quickly realise how well kids can entertain themselves without screens – and they realise that too, and often they need to appreciate it.'

Brisbane principal Catherine O'Kane says the pace of change can challenge any good parent, for before the impact of one change is obvious, more change occurs. 'Things are just moving like a freight train,' she says. 'Before you know it, you've given her a phone, but you didn't sort of think about your daughter taking a naked picture of herself when she was twelve, and then texting it. You didn't think to get in front of that.' It wasn't that parents didn't want to do the right thing; they just didn't see the wrong thing coming until it was too late.

In 2018, while chairing Queensland's Anti-Cyberbullying Taskforce, I was challenged by stories of children struggling to have their own parents switch off social media.

Dinner was late or Mum didn't hear them 'because she's on Facebook or Instagram'. Technology is increasingly the world of young parents, who have now had smartphones for more than thirteen years. Today's ten-agers have grown up in an age of technology, Professor Sanders says. 'They've probably never known a world where there hasn't been the internet. I think it is really naive to . . . assume that you can turn back the clock and all that we have to do is try to restrict screen time and we've solved the problem.' Children need to learn to navigate the online world that envelops them. 'And they need to learn to balance their access to screens and the possibilities for learning . . . with avoidance of becoming kind of obsessed and addicted to it – so that the kids can't actually function without having their phone and almost have meltdowns and panic attacks because, you know, there's some restrictions placed around its use.' If that is happening, it's a problem – but one to be managed, not avoided, he says. Some of their parents (going on the girls' responses) also need to learn that same balance.

Parenting can be stressful, even when parents work as a strong team, says Professor Sanders. 'A child is more likely to thrive if adults have reasonable expectations of what kids can do,' he says. And it runs both ways – not just understanding what is reasonable for a ten-year-old girl, but recognising that at every age we can overshoot or undershoot our child's developmental capabilities. 'Sometimes parents end up accepting what really is kind of rude and unacceptable behaviour,' he says. Many parents raise this. Children demanding what others have. Forgetting their manners, when they've spent years learning them. 'We're not doing our kids a favour by just pretending that that hasn't occurred,' Sanders says. 'If kids learn to be civil and pleasant, it's a game changer for them because adults actually want to help them and are happy to offer.' But if a ten-year-old demands something, and those demands escalate, and the parent then rewards the child by caving in, no-one wins. Professor Sanders says we also need to look after ourselves, as parents. 'Because if you're not regulating your own emotions, if you're not working as a team, if you're not doing a bit of self-care and nurturance, it's so much more difficult to be consistent and patient, positive and responsive to your kids.'

Daisy Turnbull refers to a teaching strategy called 'backwards mapping', where educators start with where they want the student to end. So in the classroom, a teacher might consider what a history student needs to learn over her years of high school, and designs the learning around that. 'Parenting should be the same,' says Turnbull. 'We don't know what our kids will be like – their personalities come out on their own and in their own time – but by having an idea of what skills we want them to have when they are teenagers, or adults, we can start working towards that goal as they grow up.'

That's when we are working together. But what about when parents are working apart. Or even against each other?

15

Parenting solo

'It is very, very difficult to separate
partnering issues from parenting issues.'

Parenting author Michael Grose

Evie and Audrey don't know each other but have so
much in common. They're both ten. Their parents are
divorced. They love sport. They both don't like the amount
of homework they're set. They love their friends, and their
pets and their parents. But all things being equal, Evie
and Audrey are on markedly different trajectories. And
that's simply a result of how their parents are dealing with
divorce. Evie's parents share custody and have set up a list
of rules that apply at both homes. She can't have a phone
in her room, for example, when she's at her mum's or her
dad's. Her bedtime is set to the same hour at both homes.

Rules about chores are the same. Routine is important. Evie's parents turn up, sometimes, at parent-teacher nights together, but if they don't, they communicate the teacher's assessment to each other. They're civil to each other, and respectful. Audrey, however, is not subject to firm rules and routines. She lives mainly with her mum, but likes visiting her dad, who lets her stay up later than her mum. He also relented and bought her a new smartphone. But she's always better prepared at her mum's: she is never without a school uniform there, she can always find her shoes, and her homework. When she's at her dad's, she's always in trouble from someone for forgetting something. She loves both of them, and they love her and tell her that. But she wishes they were still living together, in the one house. She knows that won't happen, because they talk to her about each other and she hears the nastiness in their voices when they speak at drop-off. Sometimes she wonders if it all could be her fault.

'The biggest issue is not being able to divorce the partnering from the parenting,' parenting author Michael Grose says. And when that happens, after separation, the roles get muddled. That can be difficult to understand for any ten-year-old, but it also risks forcing her to divide her loyalties. She might feel the need to take sides, or to defend one parent, or to pretend she didn't have a good time at the other's. Loving one parent feels a tad disloyal to the other; she feels as though she's betraying the other parent. Divided loyalties – 'often girls are hit by these,' Grose says. 'It's really difficult for all kids, but particularly the vulnerable age of adolescence.' School councillor Marcelle Nader-Turner says, 'A lot of the research has stated quite clearly that it's not parental separation that's the problem, it's parental conflict within that separation ... You can have parents who don't want to be together anymore but who are very capable communicators. They know their children, they know what should be shared and what shouldn't be. They keep their conflict separate.' Those children, she says, shine. 'They know they are loved. They don't see the separation as something that is their fault, which is something that happens.'

The fragility of girls struggling with parental separation can stand out. Child psychiatrist Professor James Scott says that girls appear to be much more sensitive to parental break-ups than boys. 'I very rarely see boys telling me they are feeling depressed because their parents are breaking up. Maybe they just hide it – but girls are more aware of how their parents are feeling.' This fits in with what teachers and school counsellors say: girls will talk and even canvass issues with friends more than their male peers.

Family structures and dynamics cover a broad spectrum: Dad and Mum living together and sharing parenting with all its ups and downs; Mum and Dad living together and bickering constantly; divorced parents who share parenting amicably, divorced parents who don't; single-parent families; families with two mums, families with two dads; families navigating transgender issues. Each year in Australia almost 50,000 divorces are granted, and almost half of those involve children.[1] What this project threw up was just how significant an impact a break-up has on girls – in particular, a break-up in which a soured relationship colours the parenting. Testament to this is the fact that 'family relationships' account for more calls by ten-year-old girls to Kids Helpline than any other issue.

The following comments come from tweens:

'I only see him on birthdays and Christmas.'

'I wish Dad would talk to me more.'

'I never see him to tell him that I miss him.'

'I'm closer to my step-dad.'

'Mum doesn't like me talking to him or seeing him.'

Some divorced parents are able to work together and advocate for each other. Take this instance of a father who encourages his daughter to see her mother more: 'Due to splitting of family and [older] siblings who have chosen at different times to live 100 per cent with one parent or the other, the nine-year-old is now telling her dad she wants to live with him 100 per cent. But he says it is important for him to share and [for] her to spend time with her mum.' When shared parenting like this works, the benefits are notable. 'I've interviewed parents who I didn't know until after the interview were divorced,' Sydney principal Paulina Skerman says. 'They sit in front of me and they are positive and they are civil and the child comes first.'

But that's not always the case. Other principals relate that some parents will sit in their offices and not acknowledge the other. 'That has got to be so confusing for kids,' one says, and adds: 'We have a number of students who apologise for their mothers and their fathers regularly.' She is annoyed by this. 'Why do parents use their children as pawns?' she asks. Other principals tell of parents threatening, in front of their daughter, to not fund the school fees and force her to change schools. Or to cancel permission for an upcoming excursion because of a disagreement over weekend custody. Or to deny her playing an instrument or a sport – not because they can't pay, but to niggle their ex-partner, post-break-up.

'There are split families everywhere,' one principal says, 'and I think the anxiety that causes the children can be completely destabilising, because they are so desperate to belong, they are so desperate to be part of something.' Often they take responsibility for the split, another principal says. 'Did I cause this? Have I done something wrong? What's going to happen?'

Many educators raised concerns they had during COVID, when families endured significant stress, including job losses. 'I was really worried about what some children were being exposed to at home,' one principal says. 'Those worries that a kid at that age shouldn't have to hear [like financial problems]. If she's a little girl who is the eldest, possibly – that little leader, that little responsible one – then she takes that on like [an adult].' Often schools know of an acrimonious split but have not been told by the parents. Their child reveals it. 'What is best is for parents to communicate clearly to the school what's going on, to be brave enough to say, "Unfortunately we're not getting on nicely, and can you help us work out how we can help Mary?" one principal says. It's a plea to partner with their school and put their child front and centre. 'It's really complex,' says former principal and leadership consultant Fran Reddan. But at ten children are learning to socialise, nutting out their own values and working on emotional self-regulation – and need to see those skills modelled. 'They are all really basic skills because a ten-year-old is not a mini adult. Someone's got to teach them those skills.' Teachers are an important influence here, but so are parents. 'If they are seeing fights and arguments and tension, that is really unsettling – and you see it play out in school,' she says. 'You see it in terms of their academic work, in terms of the way that they deal with the teacher, their mood. You see it with their anxiety.' Professor Scott agrees. He says he sees 'too many' children not wanting to go to school, or falling behind, because of anxiety including around parental break-ups.

Professor Matt Sanders from the Triple P Positive Parenting Program says when children become the 'meat in the sandwich' in a relationship breakdown, it means the parents have not sorted out the emotional consequences of the split. Some children ended up being 'the carrier of messages from one household to the other', he says. 'There could also be ongoing residual conflict relating to how money is spent. When you get friction, or kids arriving from one household to the other but they don't have the appropriate clothing they need – these sorts of irritations and frictions – and if children hear the adults in ongoing dispute, kids end up believing that they're the cause of relationship problems.' Crucially, they also end up believing that relationship problems don't have solutions. 'What kids need to see is adults being civil and reasonable, almost in a business-like way, after a relationship breaks down, communicating with certain ground rules.' Those ground rules, Sanders adds, need to include 'no blaming, no escalating and particularly no threatening in an environment in which children are listening'.

Judith Locke, clinical psychologist and author of *The Bonsai Child*, says, 'The main thing is try to have both households as similar as possible in terms of expectations.' She sees parents regularly feel guilt over a divorce, and then, to make up for that, alter the rules by being indulgent. That starts a chain reaction that becomes difficult to navigate: the child starts altering their behaviour because they have no boundaries, and parents attribute that to the separation – not to the fact that those boundaries have changed. 'So I think it's important to keep it predictable and routine and the same in both houses as much as you can,' Locke says. This idea is backed up by school counsellors, who applaud the manner in which some parents deal with it. Many minimise the impact on their child by ensuring they have uniforms at both homes, similar lunch boxes in both kitchens, and in some cases even duplicate textbooks. In other cases, separated parents have chosen a middle or high school in between their homes, to make travel easier for their daughter. And in others, post-break up custody deals have included the need to remain living within a reasonable distance from each other. Of course some families have this privilege and some don't. Some can afford to set up similar bedrooms and entitlements at two homes and many, many others can't. But none of that matters as much as being on the same page and upholding agreed rules and routines.

It is also vital that parents didn't wage a 'who's-the-best-parent competition', Judith Locke says. 'Kids get sucked into that very easily, because the child gets into the car and you say, "How was it at Dad's?" and they say, "The worst three days of my life." Or, "How was it at Mum's?" and they say, "Aw, she wouldn't let me get on the iPad." What often happens then is that the parents are looking for that. It's human nature,' she says. But the impact of that line of questioning can be that children feel pressured to prefer one parent over the other. Similarly, some parents will constantly contact their children while they are staying with their ex-partner. That can force a child into a difficult position, where they feel they have to show a particular loyalty.

So what happens if one parent wages an alienation strategy, despite the best efforts of the other? Experts acknowledge that this happens, and that the instigator can be either parent. Cooperation is difficult to achieve in this situation. 'You can work as hard as you can and it's not going to happen,' Judith Locke says. But she gives this analogy: children can be in one class with a teacher who has no rules, and it's mayhem. Then they can go to their next classroom with a teacher who values routine and rules and procedure, and their behaviour will change. They might be 'a little bit messy' at the beginning of the second class, but soon realise that there is a different expectation, and they rise to it. 'Each classroom can be a separate place, and kids can be different people in different homes, with different expectations – and they can learn to adjust to those different expectations,' she says. Her point is that each parent should stand firm when faced with that situation. 'When they hear that one parent has indulged [their child] and allowed them to stay up all night, there's no need to tell the child that that's terrible parenting ... Just stand firm, and keep the rules.'

It sounds easy, in theory. But in practice, relationships can be sticky, messy, full of blame and innuendo, unfair ... and a whole lot of other things. These comments are from mothers, describing how they see the relationship their daughter shares with her father.

'The relationship is strained. They don't want to visit his place for contact. He is bitter, puts me down in front of them, breaks promises and constantly lies to them.'

'She hasn't accepted her dad's choice of partner, and her father isn't able to have a relationship with her without his partner. It has resulted in refusal to see her father.'

'Her father is a narcissist and she's a people pleaser, so he's got the upper hand for now.'

'Non-existent. She stopped seeing him through the courts.'

'Her father has had very little communication or input in at least the last three years.'

'I tolerate him for the sake of my daughters. He was not a good person. But I am civil to him for their sake, and

I facilitate them seeing him and I maintain a positive facade for their sakes. My ten-year-old likes to do fun things with him (he can be quite the Disney dad) because she wants to have that similarity with her friends whose parents are not divorced. I am civil to him because she doesn't deserve to miss out on elements of having a dad.'

'He has re-partnered and has basically removed himself from her life. She is desperate to see him and spend time with him but he seems unwilling to be involved.'

However, many fathers have a different view. Repeatedly, they, and sometimes their new partners, urged me to focus on the majority of dads who desperately want to have a bigger role in their tween daughter's life. Some live heartbroken because of the limited time they get to see their children, and because of ugly partnering battles at the centre of that request. 'You tell me what I can do,' one said. 'I've tried everything.' Below are comments from fathers in similar situations.

'[My ex-wife] micromanages everything and then rings constantly when my daughter is here.'

'She finds excuses, constantly, to prevent [the kids] coming to my house.'

'I call when I'm told and then she doesn't allow me to speak to them.'

Others explained how their ex-wives had 'poisoned' their daughters against them, or how their ex-wives would make accusations at drop-off, or change the conditions of visits without any authority. Several dads pulled out photographs of their tween daughters to proudly show them off. That doesn't hide the misery writ large on their faces.

Whatever the rights and wrongs of those cases, it is the child who suffers. 'She is a girl desperately needing a positive male role model,' one mother says. And that is the case for every ten-year-old girl – whether her father is absent from her life by choice, by law or by early death. 'She lost her father young and has struggled with losing that relationship,' one mother told me. 'She craves male attention and I worry that in the future she will be taken advantage of because she is trying to replace the love that she lost when he died.'

A solid father–daughter bond is invaluable to a girl, and research has proved that over and over again. A mother is her daughter's most important role model – and a whole lot more – but a father, or father figure, can have a profound influence too. In my last book, *Fathers and Daughters*, I researched how a dad can raise a girl's academic performance, influence who she chooses as a future partner, and encourage her to take calculated risks. He can provide her with a sense of belonging, self-efficacy and resilience. He can teach her practical skills and the value of saying 'sorry', to be brave in the face of fear and to speak up for herself and others. In that previous research project, I asked girls aged eight to eighteen to nominate what they liked about their dad, and the same adjectives kept popping up: rational, hard-working, successful, organised, calm. They also love that Dad will not always solve their problems but provide alternatives when she's in a jam – and allow her to make the decision. At that younger age, around ten, they also love that he makes her feel special, that he'll jump on the trampoline and dive into the pool with her. But it's also about this time that fathers take a step back from their daughters. Sometimes it's because they want to grant her privacy, or she starts to push him away, or he is not sure how to deal with her growing adolescence and attitude. And every bit of advice I received then, and now, is for fathers not to do that. Be there. As. Much. As. Is. Possible!

Finally, we need to consider step-parents. A step-parent can be as valuable as a biological parent, a point empha-sised by parents, teachers and psychologists. One mother says this: 'I came into my [step-]daughter's life three years after her mother passed away. We have come a long way but I know her grief is endless and that I can never replace her.' This research journey has been littered with warm stories about how step-mothers and step-fathers have taken on their partner's children with gusto, respect and determination. Experts say moves to re-partner need to be taken gingerly, and with the children in mind, but our families and schools and communities are filled with children whose step-parents are their role models. In my research, girls didn't often differentiate between their parents and step-parents; what mattered was that home was a secure and nurturing place. But when they did differentiate, it was to talk of the warm bond with their step-parent.

'He's my step-dad. I know him better and am closer to him.'

'I can talk to my step-dad about anything. ANYTHING!'

Karalee Katsambanis, author of *Step Parenting with Purpose*, says step-parenting is so common now that it 'is just as important as being a parent – and sometimes even more so'. That reflects the view of every expert canvassed. It doesn't matter how families are made up, it's how they work that counts. And that comes back to Michael Grose's point: divorce the partnering from the parenting.

Divorce can also provide our children with lessons, by giving mothers and fathers the opportunity to demonstrate how to conquer personal challenges. Parenting educator Michelle Mitchell says many mothers she speaks to 'feel devastated that they couldn't give their kids the ideal and the perfect, yet what their kids really need is to see them conquer the challenges that they ... come across in life because it's that spirit that enables them to conquer their own challenges.' And it's no different for dads.

16

Nan and Pop and siblings and cousins

'Family friends and extended family play such a powerful role in our kids' lives because they give them that diversity of influence that they need.'

Parenting educator and author of *Everyday Resilience* Michelle Mitchell

Eliza's grandmother offers respite into a different world. 'She has a really big backyard and when I stay there overnight I like to wake up really, really early because Grandma wakes up at 5 am,' she says. 'She likes to sit with the birds, so we sit on the step and just watch them and listen to them and then we go for a walk in the back garden.' I'm sitting with a group of four ten-year-olds, and Eliza's tale prompts a string of others. It's an enchanting peek into the relationship between a tween and her grandparents.

'I love my nanna. She does a lot of sewing so we make a lot of creations together. I don't know anyone else who does that and she really helps me.'

'My grandad is really busy. He has his own business but he takes me everywhere with him. He's really energetic, too. We go bike riding and it's just great.'

'My grandma had a fall and she fractured her skull. But I can still talk to her and it's really easy because if I do something wrong or like I lose something, they won't get as mad as my parents.'

Four girls. Four sets of grandparents, who in many households play a vital role. Grandparents Day at schools might visibly showcase the connection between child and grandparent, but at home, and behind the scenes, grandparents are involved in an engaged and practical way. Some are footing the bill for a private education. Some are taking their children's place at parent–teacher interviews. They are babysitting, or taking children for weekends, to allow their parents some space. They play Uber driver for school sporting matches. But it's the ear they offer, and the non-judgemental support they provide, that girls say makes a measurable difference to their lives. Just listen to what our ten-year-olds say:

'Granddad is less judgemental.'

'Grandma listens to me.'

'Grandma says she will talk to Mum and make her understand for me.'

'Granddad understands me.'

'My parents think they know everything but Nan listens to what I think.'

Parenting expert Professor Matt Sanders says grandparents can also offer a valuable role when tweens are in conflict with parents. 'It's great to have an independent relationship between you as the grandparent and [your] ten-year-old [grandchild],' he says. Grandparents are able, for example, to listen to the child's perspective and troubleshoot the problem. Regular contact allows that conversation to continue, so problems are raised, discussed and often solved. This is gold for those tweens who have grandparents in their lives. Their absence during COVID stung many girls who, in addition to fearing their grandparents would die, missed that uncomplicated and regular conversation.

At schools, educators have seen the increased involvement of grandparents in volunteering, in engaging with their granddaughters and in inquiring about their class progress. In some cases, that engagement is linked to the fact that the grandparents are paying the school fees. But outside the school grounds, a good grandparent–tween relationship provides a 'white space' for girls. It's hard to find that elsewhere.

'Grandma isn't caught up in social media.'

'Grandma tells me stories about the old days.'

'Grandpa works for hours and hours on his car.'

'Grandpa works in a big bank and he didn't even like Maths at school.'

'Grandma thinks the modern world is crazy but she is so funny.'

Yes, some of them were 'crinkly', slow, frail and unable to use a smartphone, but not once, across Australia, did a ten-year-old girl say anything disparaging about the relationship they shared with the grandparents in their lives. They respected them, worried about them, missed them, wanted to have sleepovers with them . . . but their favourite pastime with grandparents was simply talking. Some girls don't have grandparents, and others have grandparents who are not in their lives (because of relationship breakdowns, for instance), but in this project it was the relationship gold they brought that was so valued.

Kevin Tutt has been a senior leader in education since 1993. He says he can see the influence of grandparents on children around the age of ten, and cites the example of the junior student leaders at Seymour College, which he headed last year. He says they both have grandparents very involves in their lives. He sees grandparents as the embodiment of two important attributes that help mould girls as they travel through adolescence and beyond: a generational perspective, and a 'values' experience. 'A grandparent can have a very different type and nature of relationship with their grandchildren,' he says. Often children demonstrate a higher level of respect than they might show others. There's also a bond of trust which sits aside from the trust they have for their parents. And a 'uniqueness about the grandparent–grandchild relationship' which allows grandparents to offer wisdom that girls were prepared to heed. Other educators agree. Toni Riordan, a Brisbane principal, says that part of the value of grandparents lies in the amount of time they afford to their grandchildren. Often they have been involved since the early years of childcare, and the relationship has grown over time. 'So we see lots of grandparents dropping girls off to training and being on the sidelines of sport – when Mum and Dad are working.' This was something almost every educator noted. 'I like to see grandparents involved,' principal Ros Curtis says. She points out that often they can be less emotional than parents, providing a strong, steadying influence within the family. 'Your first injustices tend to happen at school because you're with people. And it's at that time that you don't have your strategies to deal with them,' she says. Sometimes she's seen grandparents deal with that by providing girls with a healthy dose of perspective.

Teen psychologist Andrew Fuller says children bring 'the playfulness and joy of life into a family'. Parents were about the 'management of family' and grandparents had the role, often, 'of leadership and justice'. 'So often you can go to your grandmother or grandfather and they will provide a wise word or kindly justice,' Andrew Fuller says. 'You might not get that from Mum or Dad.' Psychologist Judith Locke says that often children will tell a story in a different way to grandparents, or others who are not their parents. 'It's interesting as a parent to hear that,' she says. The other person – let's say grandparent or aunt – doesn't take the child's news personally. 'They're not sitting there hearing that they did badly in Maths or whatever and thinking that it's because they didn't look at the homework every night. They're listening. So the child learns to tell their story in a way without judgment.'

A note here on the death of a grandparent, because for many ten-year-olds it might be the first time anyone they love has died. Judith Locke says that parents should be a little understanding of 'the different ways different children process things and some altered behaviour from them (and changing on a moment-to-moment basis).' She advises allowing 'them to grieve in the way that they want to, have them participate as much as they want to (such as going to the hospital or playing a part in the funeral, or even helping clean up their grandparent's house)'. Boundaries and normalcy make children feel safe.

Grandparents are one step removed from their grand-children: mostly, they are not resident at the home; mostly, they choose their level of involvement. And those factors also aid the relationship. It's the same with a long-time family friend, perhaps, or a favourite aunt or uncle, a teacher or sports coach, or cousins. Cousins, like grand-parents, were frequently mentioned by girls as a source of support. When asked who they would go to for help, several ten-year-olds nominated a cousin. 'I would talk to my mum and dad and my cousin, who is fifteen years old. I would tell them because I trust them very much and I know they will help me as much as they can,' one says. Another says, 'I would go to my cousins because they listen to me and have time for me.' For others, cousins provide fun and adventure, and often a ten-year-old girl will look up to her older cousin for everything from friendship to fashion advice. This is something to be encouraged and celebrated. Parenting expert Michelle Mitchell says the role played by extended families is often overlooked, but provides powerful support for girls. 'The diversity of family provides them with twenty different women, all of whom are wonderful, yet they find their fit with somebody. And I think that's just an amazing thing that we can offer,' she says. She encourages us to think about our extended family and actively pursue those alliances. 'Like the cousin who lives in Toowoomba – take a trip three times a year to see them. Just make sure they do have that real diversity,' she says.

Professor Susan Sawyer says family friends and neighbours are important in the lives of ten-year-olds. Likewise, instructors and coaches. 'Parents these days are much more likely to be fearful of the sporting coach in terms of the risk of sexually assaulting their ten-year-old – which is important to keep in mind – but fails to appreciate the tremendous opportunities that can come from the sense of pride and engagement that can be achieved,' she says. Similarly, social and emotional learning can come from a ten-year-old explaining herself to her parents' best friends. We need to be careful, she says, that we don't create a generation of children who are fearful of the external world. 'Adolescence, if all things go well, should be the time where we as humans are our most fearless, our most brave, our most prepared to push [the] boundaries that we as their parents and adults can be understandably fearful of,' she says.

Researcher Mark McCrindle says families have become far more child-centric, and that trend is continuing. 'Their grandparents were raised in an era where children were "seen and not heard", and if that wasn't a phrase prac-tised, it was a phrase that was recited. Not so for the Alphas,' he says. They are more empowered in the family unit than any generation of children before them, able to influence decision-making, from the type of car bought to the family holiday taken, and even able to dictate the design of their bedrooms. 'Children from the youngest age have their rooms set up with their choice of colours and fit-outs, rather than having to share and just having the hand-me-downs.' It's a society where we 'look down to the youth and not up to the older people', he says. That's the community at large. On a personal level, rela-tions with grandparents can be as endearing as they are encouraging.

No account of the significant relationships in a ten-ager's world is complete without mentioning siblings. There is no doubt that a ten-year-old's relationship with her siblings shapes the person she will become. At ten and eleven, the time siblings spend alone with each other is 2.8 hours each weekday and 5.9 hours on weekend days. This later declines to 1.8 hours each weekday and 3.4 hours each weekend day by the ages of fourteen and fifteen,[1] but the fact remains that siblings spend a lot of time together, whatever the age. School principal Toni Riordan says she sees the importance of a sibling relationship in her own life, being the elder sibling and having a younger sister. 'That sister relationship is what has shaped my life,' she says. In her case, being a big sister taught her leadership skills. Her parents were small business owners, and the girls would independently get themselves off to school and fill the hours each weekend. Now, both of them would acknowledge that the roles they played with each other have kitted them out with the skills they hold dear.

Andrew Fuller says we are defined by each other and our parents. 'So if you're a ten-year-old girl and you're the youngest child in a family with, say, four older brothers, you could be the cherished girl,' he says. That could result in a sense of disempowerment or strength, depending on the role the girl plays. So how do siblings know what role to play? Fuller uses a baseball game analogy, but experience has shown him that you can't be too prescriptive. 'A kid comes along and says to the other siblings, you've got that covered so I won't do that, I'll do this instead.' That means one child might play the guitar and another will deliberately *not* take up the guitar. Or it might relate to sport. But each finds a 'base' for themselves. The role they play in each other's development is huge, but each comes from a different perspective. 'That's why when you get adults together and they'll compare family stories, they can be completely different stories.' They play different roles, and see things differently.

Principal Ros Curtis says every time she sees a pattern emerge, she finds another example where it's not the case.

It is easy to stereotype – for example, the bossy oldest child, the needy middle child, the spoilt baby – but it doesn't always play out like that. 'I've seen plenty of examples of that, but I've also seen where the eldest might be a bit off the rails, the middle child is the one who has it sorted, and the youngest child is flying by, keeping the whole family together.' She says that each time a girl is made school captain she worries slightly. She worries about the impact on her siblings, but has learnt it really depends on the family dynamic and the messages she is given. That focus on family messaging and parenting 'values' drives former Seymour College principal Kevin Tutt's responses. He says older sisters, for example, can be bad role models or wonderful ones. It comes down to the family and how they value each daughter's contribution.

Professor Matt Sanders makes the point that there is no other relationship a ten-year-old will have for so long as the sibling relationship. 'It really, really, really pays to get on well with your siblings,' he says. If the relationship was coloured by bitterness or resentment in its early days, conflict could last a lifetime. Some of the worst bullying occurs in families, Sanders says. 'Sibling bullying is a real problem and it's linked to bullying with peers – but the point that I'm making here is that those soured relationships with siblings can last a lifetime.' He urges parents to remember that a sibling relationship is a prototype of peer relationships: how children interacted with each other, how they shared, how they spoke to each other, and whether they engaged in physical violence. He urges parents to consider two issues. 'One is, what are the social skills that I want my kids to learn when they're engaging with each other? For example, if you want a turn at something, how do you ask, and if someone has asked you, how do you respond?' And second, when children are being hurtful and disrespectful, it is important for parents to 'call it out'. 'It needs to be a ground rule that we speak to each other in a different way or we speak to each other civilly in this household, and just to ignore it or to say "kids will be kids" basically leaves you as the parent feeling as though you've got no influence whatsoever, when in fact there's a lot you can do to make a big difference to how siblings get on with each other.' He says when sibling conflict occurs – and that is at the heart of much of the family conflict he sees – parents need to enact a plan and a strategy to deal with it.

Part of this, says Kevin Tutt, is for parents to resist their second or third child's requests for material items or privileges that their elder siblings have. 'It should be, "You don't get a mobile phone until you're twelve – that's the rule and that's how we're doing it in this family." Tutt, like many educators, says the difference in age between siblings is often ignored by parents. Often the eldest daughter might have received a smartphone at thirteen but her parents will be worn down and grant her eleven-year-old sister the same privilege. The same with make-up. And bedtimes. And attending parties.

Toni Riordan says an acknowledgement of the bond between sisters was a significant school celebration at her all-girls' school in Year 12s, when students are about to leave their last assembly. 'One of the recurring agenda items of that assembly is what we call the Sister Act. And that's where the little sisters of the big sisters who are leaving put together a song and they have flowers and they actually say something – and they all cry.' What they say to their older sister delights staff. 'It goes from practical things like "I'm going to miss you driving me to school every day" to "It was so comforting to know that you were always here".' The role of a sibling, particularly an older sister, surfaced several times in the responses of girls. 'My sister is around my age so she knows what to do,' one says, and adds, 'She is also very kind.' Another says, 'I would go to my sisters with a problem because I trust them.' And another: '[I turn to] my sister because she understands that I am having a hard time.'

Michael Grose, author of *Why First-Borns Rule the World and Last-Borns Want to Change it*, says the impact of siblings is underestimated. 'We overestimate, in some ways, the impact of parents. Sibling relationships will outlast the parent–child relationship. And in days gone by, when families were large, it was siblings who did a lot of the child rearing. Parents tended to be delegators.'

He says siblings, particularly girls, learnt to quasi-parent. 'So if you've got a ten-year-old girl and a thirteen- to fourteen-year-old girl, there's a reasonable chance that that thirteen- to fourteen-year-old girl will be sort of a nurturing type, if she's been given the chance. And she'll be a positive role model.' She will also have two 'faces' he says – one for her friends, allowing her to be a fourteen-year-old, and one she wears at home, where she is more the nurturer.

Professor Sanders says it's important for children to look for the value in both their big sisters and their big brothers. The way they do this might be more nuanced than seeking advice. 'It's about watching what they do, watching how they handle themselves,' he says. Those who take the time to listen to their younger sister – or brother – and see themselves as a role model or mentor develop strong attributes themselves. 'But you can't get preachy and moralistic with it, because that's a big turn-off,' he warns older siblings. While no simple formula exists for how siblings bond, it is worth focusing on. 'Sibling relationships actually affect achievement, affect your capacity to keep out of trouble. [They affect] many aspects of your own personal wellbeing.'

So what happens if your ten-year-old daughter doesn't get on with her siblings? 'I think sometimes the harder the kids fight, as long as it's not toxic, then the harder they love each other,' Michael Grose says. 'You practise all sorts of relationship skills on your siblings. You practise being assertive, you practise ducking and weaving from them, you practise compromise. You do a lot of things that you put into place in other relationships, whether it's at school or relationships later on in life.' Michael Grose says he had three children and his daughters used to 'fight like cats and dogs when they were young'. But they also fiercely looked out for each other. Now, in their thirties, their relationship is prized.

It takes a village to raise a child, and brothers and sisters, aunts and uncles, grandparents and cousins all hold a very special place in that village.

That COVID monster

'If I had a magic wand, I'd give them the confidence
... to be positive about the future for themselves.'

Karen Spiller, principal, John Paul College

Anna's mother is a GP. Each day, as the coronavirus reached its tentacles into communities across the world, she would go to work, a suburb away from where she lived. Her husband had become part of the at-home workforce, and her two children, ten and fourteen, sat at the kitchen table, learning online. 'I loved that my dad finally stayed home and I got to know him for the first time in my life,' says Anna. But the judgement she delivers on her mother is crushing. What she remembers most, she says, is that her mother would arrive home and not hug her – or at least, not until she'd had a shower.

It's one story, but it showcases the thoughts of so many of our ten-year-olds. In the first place, kids found a silver lining in the pandemic: they got to spend more time with their fathers. Not able to work from the office, being at home allowed dads the opportunity to engage in a game of cards, a bike ride after work and dinner together every night. Long conversations replaced many of the short procedural chats on the drive between home and school. Girls noticed this, and raised it without prompting: Dad was home. Dad had dinner with us every night. Dad and I did this. Dad and I did that. Mostly Mum helped with their schoolwork – without the same recognition! Which brings me to my second point. In many cases, where Mum worked outside the home in an essential service, girls delivered harsh judgements on their mothers. 'She chose them [people who required testing], not me,' Anna says. 'She was at work testing and looking after people, and my sister and I had to look after ourselves.'

This is an interesting insight into biases, but more significantly it's an insight into how some of our ten-year-olds saw – and continue to see – the coronavirus as a threat to their safety and security. For some children, the initial weeks of lockdown provided a wonderful pause in a busy schedule, a welcome chance for parents to engage with them in a different way, and even a pathway to a more secure school day (more on that later). But for many children, lockdown was, and remains, plain scary.

That's understandable. The uncertainty that surrounded 2020 led to behaviour that was unsettling. Fights over toilet paper in the supermarket aisle. School shut. Sport cancelled. Dance cancelled. Parks closed. Drinking fountains closed. Friends and grandparents out of bounds. And the unpredictability of what all these things meant for them and their families. For many, it delivered increased anxiety, difficulty in sleeping and too many nightmares. GPs reported that. So did psychologists. And schools too were on high alert for those children, learning remotely, who were struggling with more than the class lesson. Teachers saw it when girls returned to school – in their writing, in the pictures they drew: a big black monster watching the family from the lounge-room window, or a hulking figure knocking at the door.

'At the end of this pandemic, will life ever go back to normal again, and when family are sick, will they ever get better?' That's one question posed by a ten-year-old girl. 'I was scared,' another says. Others told of their inability to sleep unless one of their parents was lying in bed with them, how they cried because they didn't want to do school at home, how they missed their friends and wondered whether they'd ever see them again, how they missed their grandparents and their teachers and their playground and their sports, how they had to withdraw from theatre and ballet and scouts, and how they worried that their family – mostly their mother – might die. Numerous studies both here and overseas pointed to increases in anxiety, stress and depression, and the need for that to be addressed. One study, by UNICEF Australia, found that only 52 per cent of boys and 38 per cent of girls aged thirteen to seventeen were coping well in mid-2020.[1] It is unlikely to have been much different for ten-year-olds.

The struggles girls had with COVID were raised by many parents. Here's a handful of comments representative of so many of the concerns of mothers with tween girls.

'She does not want us to use the word "corona" anymore.'

'She is lonely but doesn't know how to reach out to her friendship groups. She is concerned about the world ending and never having achieved.'

'I'm in treatment for breast cancer so she's worried I will die if I get the virus.'

'I'm a doctor so I'm working huge hours and often exhausted. She is envious of her friends who have their mums at home.'

'She has cried a lot over this. She is afraid our family might get it.'

'She keeps going over and over the problems (i.e. Why would someone eat a bat?).'

'She was very upset the Easter bonnet parade was cancelled. She has made some badges saying "Corona Virus Survivor".'

'We noticed the other day – she was very sad and glum. It was the first time we have ever seen this characteristic in her. We asked if she wanted to talk to a friend but she said that she had nothing to say.'

'Initially she refused to talk or listen to anything about it and would become quite hysterical. Eventually we managed to get her to talk, and she believed that if you got it, you died. We've cleared that up.'

'She was washing her hands so much they were cracking and bleeding. She wasn't sleeping because she caught a cough and kept panicking that she had COVID. She's scared about getting it because I have a chronic illness.'

'We didn't realise tutorials she was watching [for an online game] had ads [with] COVID content, and the YouTubers were talking about it too. She couldn't escape it and got overwhelmed.'

Themes developed: of missed rites of passage, like school trips to Canberra and leadership ceremonies; missed birthday parties; upset routines; worries because Mum or Dad had lost their jobs. Daughters, according to experts, seemed to worry about these things more than sons.

Outbursts of tears, and a decline in social skills, were also raised repeatedly during the online teaching period. A dip in motivation – including with schoolwork – also popped up. Less common, but significant enough to raise, were cases of girls refusing to go to school once the classrooms reopened.

Professor Sarah Blunden, the head of paediatric sleep research and a lecturer in clinical psychology at Central Queensland University, says part of the problem is the lack of control children – and adults – had with this pandemic. 'It's not just about sleeping. It's about everything,' she says. 'But when you are lying in bed at night, trying to sleep, and you've got less activity going on in your brain and your body, what's going to come in? What are you thinking about? Worries. And what are you going to worry about? The most relevant thing on everybody's mind. And ten-year-olds are going to be struggling much more than you or me.'

An important point here: for some children, school closures and isolation must have proved even more traumatic. Jon Rouse, the head of Taskforce Argos, says that the 'number of actual reports of sexual and physical abuse to children dropped by about 40 per cent during COVID, and the logical reason for that is the children weren't able to do their normal reporting.' Before the pandemic, 'They might go to school and they have bruising, or they go to school and they disclose to a friend, or to a teacher.' But during lockdown, these children were cut off from that vital support network. The fall-out of this is still to be seen.

Other children found the new 'norm', prompted by school closures, a delight. Sleep-ins, no early rush out the door, no long bus trips to school, watching movies at night, playing board games, learning to cook, engaging with their parents and siblings in a new way. 'I actually think our children have rekindled their sibling relationships during our time in self-isolation and they've been getting along really well,' one parent says. Many parents also used 2020 to provide their ten-year-old with a dose of independence. In many cases children were permitted to choose their own bedtime or given a smartphone to keep in contact with friends. Both of those will pose ongoing challenges. Parents also say they increased pocket money for extra jobs, like cooking dinner, and allowed their daughters to wear the regulation school uniform top, but with pyjama bottoms, during online classes.

For many children, the closures provided a boost to their schoolwork. For example, several educators believe it allowed quieter girls to have a bigger say in class discussions without feeling as though the eyes of the class were upon them. This led to better results. In other cases, parents reported a drop in anxiety: home provided a sanctuary away from friendship fights, competition and the argy-bargy of the school day. 'She is thriving as a result,' one mother says. 'The decreased stress and pressure and no school have meant that we've seen a marked difference in behaviour and tantrums.' While that observation was echoed by many, hundreds of mothers, especially, found it almost impossible for their children to learn and for them (the parents) to work at the same time. You can't set all ten-year-olds up at the kitchen table and ask them to read the required material and answer the questions while you pop into the room next door for an online meeting. This was missed in the debate over lessons from home, and coloured the potential of home time for many families. For other parents, it provided a glimpse into the learning world of their children – and where they believed their child needed attention. School after school has been approached by parents demanding teachers change their teaching to address that. Close to 90 per cent of Australians kept their children home during the first COVID outbreak. And according to Mark McCrindle's 2020 *The Future of Education* report, the experience was ultimately labelled by 71 per cent of Australian households as a positive one.[2]

Despite the disruption to routine, many ten-year-olds took to school easily on return. 'It has been an absolute delight seeing the girls come back after COVID-19 and play,' Brisbane principal Toni Riordan said after the first wave. 'I really think that it's probably tipped the scales. I think there was so much computer activity that they were abso-lutely sick of it, so just to come back and run around . . .

there's been massive games of Tiggy or Red Rover across Year levels. So that's been an absolute silver lining.'

But how will our girls be as we move forward, and as third waves and unemployment levels and vaccines dominate discussion? How will 2020 affect our tweens in 2021 and 2022 and beyond, as they continue to climb through high school? And what did schools and families learn, during challenging times, that might make that climb easier and more enjoyable? Melbourne deputy principal Kellie Lyneham says schools continue to look at – and deal with – the increased use of technology. 'As educators, we need to strategically think about the impact that this has had on all our girls, particularly this kind of tween and pre-teen age who've had iPads thrust into their hands without us really doing any preparation,' she says. With a tween-aged child of her own, she's speaking as a parent as well as an educator. She says her family thought they had a couple of years to establish how they would allow technology and the parameters around it, but COVID-19 and online learning took that away. This pandemic might have first made headlines at the end of 2019, but the small print will be written for years. 'Patterns have been created in homes, including mine, where [device] use has become normal. And we have to now understand the impact of those patterns on the children's development, and then [as educators] give parents the tools to try to wind some of [that impact] back.'

Others agree strongly. It's natural that parents might find it difficult to step in and remove computers, iPads and smartphones after the immediate need for those devices has passed. They are often afraid that their child might miss out, or be unhappy, or be singled out by others. Kellie Lyneham asks the question: Do we say 'no' enough to our kids? 'It's quite hard, particularly in this kind of environment when everything else has been taken away. I think probably the push needs to be helping parents to kind of reset the playing field, post-COVID, for parenting.'

Across Australia, the advice on how to deal with the pandemic, going forward, is similar for both parents and educators. Listen to our children. Provide ten-year-olds with a level of control, to balance out the uncertainty that fills the news. And be honest about what we have learnt. Sydney principal Paulina Skerman says that 'the world can be frightening for little people'. 'We need to be really mindful of exposing them to things and showing them how they can have some control over that situation, rather than letting them be overwhelmed. So whatever we do has to be little steps where they've got some traction in making a difference,' she says.

Going forward, it's also important to identify the positives that blossomed during 2020, including how children now see hygiene, for example. Lisa Miller, head of a Melbourne junior school, says the positives need to be nurtured. 'There's so many . . . The children have been able to learn about the technology in a way they never would have,' she says. 'And – this won't be the same for everyone – but they got to spend time home with their family, they got to go to school with their pyjama bottoms and have their shirt on top, they got to spend more time with their pets and have a restful time and work out that they don't need to be so busy. We have to focus on those.' She says the full emotional impact of this generation, coined 'the COVID kids' – won't be known for five or ten years. Children are intelligent and resourceful, she says, and 'the more we treat them like that, the better they are'. That means filtering what they see, but not hiding COVID and its aftermath from them. We need to talk to them about it. They need to feel safe.

Lessons abound for schools, too, and many of those are being trialled in classrooms across the country now. Indeed, 60 per cent of teachers surveyed agreed that the epidemic had created 'a positive disruption to the current school system'.[3] But no-one believes schooling, into the future, can trot along the same as it has for decades. Home schooling, or learning online, showed up shortcomings in the system, and encouraged new ways of looking at a child's education. Individual and personalised learning tops the list, with educators, researchers and academics all poring over data about how different students engaged with lessons during school closures. Some students – particularly those who are shy – shone. Girls who sat in the middle of the class, academically, lifted. Louder girls struggled, with educators noting that these girls felt 'lost without an audience'. Some girls who are normally very socially engaged at school found returning to class difficult after the first lengthy break. Teachers across the nation – in public and private schools – recorded a drop in social skills, particularly among nine- and ten-year-olds. Girls didn't know how to talk to each other in person. Other teachers found girls returned with a dent in their confidence. Others had a confidence boost. It became apparent that some girls thrive on the structure of a classroom, others become 'invisible'. The bottom line is that no unifying theme developed – except that children learn differently, at different times and in different ways – and any innovation in education going forward needs to require both flexibility and an individual focus.

Gold Coast principal Susan Dalton says she saw gains in those students sitting on Bs and Cs. 'They became more engaged through remote learning. One thing we've learned is we probably haven't looked deep enough or trusted the kids enough to actually guide their own learning.' Many blossomed without too much direct instruction. She says teachers also were more open-minded as to how students could learn, and suggests that future classes should encourage blended models of learning. Another principal says at-home learning helped the 'organised, the structured and the introverted'. At many schools, now, timetables are being reimagined, particularly for students in Years 11 and 12, and staff and student discussions are looking at flexibility in learning and how subjects are taught. Brisbane principal Toni Riordan says she loves the idea of cutting through the rigidity of learning at home vs learning at school to provide a different way of educating that might include both. 'It will mean a genuine review of our calendar and our school calendar and it will mean a genuine look and a reimagining of timetables,' Riordan says. 'Across the board now there's a fast-growing movement to personalise or individualise learning. I think we've been talking about it in schools for the last decade, but it's finally hit that we actually have to do it.' Schools need to know each student, provide for a bigger student voice, and customise learning plans. One small understanding, she says, resulted in the introduction of a 'consolidation day' during the school shutdown period, and that proved a game-changer. 'We knew that the girls were tired [of] being on the computer, and teachers were setting a lot of work and they didn't have that opportunity to monitor how much that was.' So every two weeks, one day was set aside where no new work was set, and teachers were on standby if students had questions. It allowed students to stand back and assess where they were, what they understood and where they needed assistance.

The push for individualised learning is understandable. It's the way of the world, 'from story books to advertising', says Mark McCrindle. 'It is likely that in the coming years education will follow suit.' More than a third of parents and a quarter of educators believe schools should provide individualised education for all students. It's a noble goal, but is it realistic? Mark McCrindle found that seven in ten parents believe it is, compared with 55 per cent of educators.[4] 'Expectation gaps such as this can become areas of conflict if not addressed. It is important for schools to communicate effectively about their ability to provide individualised education,' he says. But in all the excitement about the future learning of our ten-year-olds, equity issues present an enormous hurdle. Take this example. At one city school, ten-year-olds were given a computer, detailed daily online lessons, and regular video check-ins with their teacher. At another school, less than 8 kilometres away, teachers were photocopying lessons and driving their own cars to students' homes to drop the lessons off.

Experienced Adelaide educator Kevin Tutt says the pandemic taught him that we live in a complex and uncertain world, and that subsequently 'our leadership needs to be different. There's a new normal, and that will keep changing. We've got to be increasingly flexible. Communication has to be so much better. We need to be more resilient, because all those wonderful consistencies have gone.' Increased health literacy in primary school and more collaborative peer teaching have also been encouraged – and adopted – by others.

Other principals raise new learning pathways. One big Melbourne school is looking at combined face-to-face and distance learning for girls on the autism spectrum, after finding they blossomed during at-home schooling. Several have revamped their social-emotional learning programs, with an increased emphasis on both self-regulation and resilience. This is particularly the case for those around the age of ten. Previous studies, in the US and New Zealand, have shown children were not disadvantaged academically after natural disasters forced school closures. It is true that other studies have shown the opposite, but those standing in front of the classroom believe the bigger challenge – with ten-year-olds – has proved to be around social connection and grit. 'I really wanted to say to parents – but I couldn't – "If [your children] miss six months of schooling it's no big deal,"' one middle school teacher says. 'At the end of the day, we needed them to feel connected. That is our aim.' At this age, and often at a new middle school, children need to bond with friends, navigate different groups, understand routines, and find themselves. The pandemic that closed schools in 2020 cancelled that and, at the same time, created a new reliance on technology and increased screen time. Today, teachers and schools have had to ramp up socialisation programs to address the fall-out.

18

What our ten-agers want to tell us

'I have big hopes for this generation.
I feel privileged raising her.'

A mother

The words are written on scraps of paper, torn from notebooks:

'Dear Mum and Dad, I love you a lot but I wish you wouldn't cut me off when I'm talking. Also some more privacy please.'

'Can I have a phone and can you spend more time with me?'

'Can you listen to me without commenting and [then forgetting what I said] completely?'

'Can we do more things with family including Dad because he is always at work?'

Their authors are sitting around a school table in front of me. They look remarkably similar. Most have ponytails, set high. They are all wearing the same uniform, and their eyes sparkle with the challenge of answering the question in front of them. Some start doodling on the paper; perhaps they are working up the courage to tell it how it is. *What do you really want from your parents?* The answers, like the girls themselves, are strikingly similar. Despite their different upbringings and home lives, their different challenges and dreams, our ten-agers want time. Time to talk and do things and be listened to, without judgement. They want more privacy and more independence, but they desperately want Mum and Dad as their wingmen and women on the road to adolescence. 'I want Mum to listen to me when I am asking her to do something, but she's working on a screen,' one says. 'I wish she could hang out with me more and not stress so much. She is so hard-working and needs to have a rest.' They want different things, often, from Mum and from Dad, but that plea to be heard is to both parents.

Consider these answers to the question, What do you love your mother doing with you?

'Going shopping and watching movies together, but we rarely do that as she's always too busy.'

'I love it when me and my mum go shopping together and when she has a happy moment with me.'

'I love cooking with my mum and helping her. I also like making her day really nice.'

'Hugs and kisses and lots of love and playing games and teaching her cringe dances.'

'I love Mum and I singing together in the car every afternoon.'

'I love when my mum takes me out for afternoon tea, and I also love it when I hug Mum.'

'Because I have lots of sisters it is hard for me to get time to be with my mum, but I love it just being us and not my sisters with her.'

'I love my mum sitting with me in bed to give me comfort and her giving me lots of hugs and telling me she loves me.'

'Actually talking to me and not [being] on her phone.'

That last answer was provided a surprising number of times, given that so many parents express concern about their children's use of technology. But wishing Mum wasn't so attached to her phone was the only negative response uncovered in the 500 answers to that question. Our ten-year-olds love cosying up to us on the couch, going to the cinema with us, chatting in bed with us on a Sunday morning, spending an afternoon at the shops together, going out for hot chocolates, trying out a new recipe with us, and having us braid their hair or read them a story.

So what do our ten-agers wish us mums would do more of? These are the most common answers:

'Complain less about my messy room.'

'Hug me when I come home from school.'

'Let me finish my sentences instead of talking over me.'

'Trust me more.'

'Hang out with me, just the two of us.'

'Cook with me.'

'Spend more time with me and not worry about work.'

'I wish my mum would not go to work as much as she does.'

'I wish my mum worked less.'

'Snuggle and rest more and shut the office early.'

'Just listen, rather than give advice.'

'I wish my mum would let me have more freedom and not to take my music practice too seriously.'

The answers are heartwarming and heartbreaking in equal measure. They all want more of what they love most from their mums. Those hugs at the end of a school day. A chance to talk and be listened to. No overseas holidays, no visits to big theme parks, no extravagant requests. Indeed, almost all answers came down to two things: time, and the touch involved in snuggles and cuddles and kisses. Our ten-agers want a reminder that they remain the centre of our worlds.

Of course there are other things: to take their side and not their brother's in arguments, and even to drink more wine! '[I wish] Mum would drink wine more often because she always is in a good mood when she drinks wine.' They also wish she'd work less outside the home or not at all. Many girls said, without prompting, that they wished their mother 'didn't have to work' so she could be at home. That answer, tellingly, wasn't quite the same when the girls were asked about their fathers (more on that later).

Our tweens love spending time with Dad, even if they don't always show it.

> 'I love playing table tennis and going bike riding because he is really good at it, and with table tennis it is always tight.'

> 'Playing with him.'

> 'Giving me hugs and tickling me before bed.'

'We love talking about music together and I like showing him my compositions. We like talking about sport and sometimes Dad, my sister and I like to go to the park to play footy.'

'I love playing chess and watching funny movies but most of all I love when he tells me funny stories.'

'Building things in the garage like sawing things out of wood and making spears with an axe.'

'I love my dad and I going bike riding and kayaking.'

'I like anything as long as he visits me.'

'A game we made up called "a hunt for tickles" and it's where my dad hunts me down and tries to tickle me.'

'When he isn't just talking about business, or playing video games, and sits down with his family and we all have a good laugh.'

Juggling and rock climbing, playing touch, building stuff, bike-riding, taking the dogs for a walk, skateboarding, playing tag or hide and seek, playing basketball, kicking the ball at the park, going camping. Activities headed the list of what our ten-agers love to do with their dads – and it's good for both of them. Research shows that involving fathers in an exercise program with their daughters leads to increased activity in both girls and fathers, increased physical competence in girls, improved parenting practices in fathers, and even decreased screen time for girls and fathers.[1]

What do they wish their dads would do more of?

'Spend more time together because he only gets Sunday off because he is the boss of his work.'

'I wish he would not have to stress so much even though he has a lot to stress over. I wish he could spend a bit more time with me and my family.'

'Dance with me.'

'I don't have a father, but I wish I did.'

'I wish my dad would not take my sports too seriously because sometimes I feel like fainting when I run too much.'

'Turn his phone off.'

'I wish my dad would take me camping more often. And I wish he would play basketball in the driveway with me more often.'

Like Mum, our tweens want Dad to 'get off his phone' and 'go on more daddy–daughter dates'. While some boasted they had 'the best dad I could ever ask for', others bemoaned the fact that he wasn't in their lives. 'I'd like my dad to want to see me,' one said. They want their father to play with them more, and to be home more. None of them asked him not to work – but many wanted Dad to work fewer hours, be home earlier, and dine with the family more. It's busyness at work that they believe steals time away from being with them.

The plea for more time with both Mum and Dad is similar, but we shouldn't underestimate the difference between wanting Mum not to work and wanting Dad to work less. This demonstrates how many young women – even at ten – view the role of men and women at work in different ways.

School counsellor Marcelle Nader-Turner can remember when her own mother started working, when she was ten. 'She'd been an at-home mum all that time, and I can remember when she started working because we'd get home from school and there weren't fresh biscuits on the bench, or if it was raining we'd have to walk [home]!' she recalls. Nader-Turner wonders if girls' views on their mother working differed depending on whether their mum had always worked, or had decided to rejoin the paid workforce when their child was closer to ten. 'If a ten-year-old girl's mum suddenly starts going to work, I think the answer would be different to one whose mum has always been at work,' she says. 'I'm thinking that the ones whose mums have always been at work have probably felt a little bit absent. So the need and the want for that closeness is kind of like a hunger versus the ten-year-old girl whose mother suddenly goes to work – she's full of all of those cuddles and time. Her bank account is full.'

'Ten-year-old girls are clearly very impacted by the social creations of our gender expectations,' Nader-Turner says. 'Dad is the one who does the easy stuff. The carefree stuff, throws me round. Mum does the driving around, the problems, when things aren't working at school or whatever. Dad is the entertainment officer.' But it's less a gender issue and more likely to be about the non-primary parent, she says. 'I know people who have the roles around the other way – Dad's been an at-home dad and Mum's been working, and Dad immediately loses the entertainment officer status because he's got to do all that stuff – like, 'Where's your lunch box?''

Leadership consultant and former principal Fran Reddan says ten-agers, aware of a mother's innate guilt, might choose to play on it. Daisy Turnbull, an author and teacher, says there is plenty of guilt associated with being a mother – both working-mother guilt and stay-at-home-mother guilt. 'Parenting, especially [for] mothers, seems to have more guilt associated with it than a confessional,' she says.

School principal Karen Spiller raises another issue that arises between girls and their mothers, and is an inevitable part of growing up. She says that in the lead-up to this age, mothers and daughters usually share a treasured bond. 'You can do no wrong in her eyes, and then somewhere around eight or nine it can start to go a bit awry.' This is when a girl might turn away from her family being her whole world and focus instead on outside influences, like peers and popular culture. She wants desperately not to be her mother, or desperately to be her mother. 'If you are incredibly successful in one particular area, the daughter will often rebel against that because [she doesn't] think [she] can reach the high standards of her mother,' Spiller says. A daughter might avoid a certain interest or subject out of fear she won't 'cut it' in comparison to her mother.

The plea for more time is directed at both parents, and the amount of time young people spend with them declines substantially between the ages of ten to eleven and fourteen to fifteen. The Longitudinal Study of Australian Children (LSAC) found that, between ages ten and eleven, the average amount of time spent with parents was 2.6 hours each weekday and 5.4 hours each Saturday and Sunday. By age fourteen to fifteen, this fell to 2.2 hours on weekdays and 4.3 hours on weekends. It also showed that children spent considerably more time with their mother than with their father, particularly on weekdays. It is significant to note that the work hours of both parents didn't have a major impact on the total amount of time that adolescents spent with their parents. 'The only significant difference was that adolescents spent an average of 14 minutes less per day with their parents if their mother worked full-time hours, rather than being not employed,' it says. And on average, girls spent 11 minutes more per day with their mothers than boys did, but boys spent 20 minutes more each day with their fathers.[2] Another analysis of that LSAC data found 70 per cent of children aged ten to eleven enjoyed spending time with their mothers and fathers – compared with just over 50 per cent at ages fourteen and fifteen.[3]

Michelle Mitchell, parenting educator and author of *Everyday Resilience*, wonders if children's needs might extend beyond simply more time with Mum and Dad. 'I just wonder these days if there's so many other influences on the family unit that what Mum and Dad do doesn't necessarily mean the outcome we want. Just say kids got all the hugs, cuddles and time in the world – is that going to make them feel stronger? More resilient? I don't know,' she says. 'It's very difficult to shelter kids from the fast-paced life and the stress that they're living in. And I'm not sure more cuddles and hugs are going be able to [do that].' She says consistency is king, but acknowledges that it can be difficult to 'be so consistent when [parents are] juggling 50 billion things ... A lot of the time the finger is pointed at parents and they're busting their guts for their kids – but the world they're living in is working against them.' Sometimes parents deserve a break and need to focus on what they're doing right, rather than listen to others claiming what they're doing wrong.

Psychologist Judith Locke adds another important point to this discussion, and that is that sometimes parents step back – particularly fathers. 'Definitely fathers do start stepping back from their child when they start to get a little bit more awkward, get a little bit bigger, you know, not fit in comfortably next to them on the couch and things like that.' Sometimes parents are hurt by their daughter confiding secrets in their friend, or no longer always downloading their day in the way they did a couple of years earlier. 'Parents are human and they can react that way as well,' Locke says. 'I think often in their quest to give their child independence, it's just very hard to get the balance right.' That balance points to what Judith Locke sees as the biggest challenge for ten-year-old girls: successfully individuating from their parents. That entails managing the change from being totally reliant on parents to understanding the role of friends and the influence of the outside world. Parents need to walk a similar tightrope: allowing their daughters gradual independence and stopping back slowly, to encourage less reliance, more autonomous decision-making and the wonder delivered by good friendships. Locke advocates negotiating time with children and spending it on activities that are project-based – like cooking or gardening. 'Sometimes that doesn't make the conversations as intense; it's almost like play, which makes it easier for children to confide in you, too.'

Most of the 500 girls in this project, along with the 1600 mums, 400 dads and 100 teachers, are privileged. The girls go to school – many attend private colleges and public schools where the opportunities rival their dreams. Most say they feel loved and looked after. None said they were homeless. Certainly some had suffered serious illness, but all had had access to care. A chunk of them would be struggling with the evils of child abuse, which should never be underestimated. But a sense of perspective is important too. In some communities in other countries, girls aged ten are near being married off, and others are forbidden any sort of education. That doesn't mean the problems our girls articulate should be underestimated or downplayed. Leadership consultant Fran Reddan, who previously ran Melbourne Girls Grammar, says girls want us to 'pay attention, not pay for things'. And that has been underpinned by almost every answer, from every girl. They want to love their friends and learn to love themselves. They want to feel strong and capable. They want to walk with the confidence they did a couple of years earlier, when they didn't know they were being watched. They want to be leaders and learners, without feeling anxiety is suffocating their day. Sometimes, they say, it's hard to tell their parents these things. But when they jot it down, in the handwriting of a fierce girl on the way to awesome womanhood, it's our time and our touch that they think will help most. 'People need to know that they're valued,' Fran Reddan says, 'and there's something about that physical connection of the hug and cuddle that brings comfort and confidence.' It's a gift, no matter our circumstances, that we can all afford.

Endnotes

Chapter 2

1. Dunn, A 2017, *The New Puberty*, Melbourne University Press, Melbourne, p. 41.

Chapter 3

1. Oprah Winfrey Network 2015, *The lesson Brené Brown's daughter learned about trust*, online video, 6 November, YouTube, <https://www.youtube.com/watch?v=6442YcvEUH8>.

Chapter 4

1. Internet Watch Foundation 2020, 'Millions of attempts to access child sexual abuse online during lockdown', <https://www.iwf.org.uk/news/millions-of-attempts-to-access-child-sexual-abuse-online-during-lockdown>.
2. Internet Watch Foundation 2020, '"Terrifying escalation" in battle to keep children safe online as new figures reveal 300,000 people in the UK could pose sexual threat to children', <https://www.iwf.org.uk/news/'terrifying-escalation'-battle-to-keep-children-safe-online-as-new-figures-reveal-300-000>.
3. Australian Bureau of Statistics 2018, 'Household use of information technology', <https://www.abs.gov.au/ausstats/abs@.nsf/mf/8146.0>.

Chapter 5

1. eSafety Commissioner n.d., 'Cyberbullying', Australian Government, <https://www.esafety.gov.au/key-issues/cyberbullying>.
2. Queensland Anti-Cyberbullying Taskforce 2018, *Adjust Our Settings: A community approach to address cyberbullying among children and young people in Queensland*, Queensland Government, Brisbane, p. 3, <https://campaigns.premiers.qld.gov.au/antibullying/taskforce/assets/anti-cyberbullying-taskforce-final-report.pdf>.
3. eSafety Commissioner, 'Cyberbullying'.
4. Kids Helpline data sought and provided specifically for this research project.

Chapter 6

1. Kay, K & Shipman, C 2018, *The Confidence Code for Girls*, HarperCollins, New York, p. 10.

Chapter 7

1. Van Cuylenburg, H 2019, *The Resilience Project: Finding happiness through gratitude, empathy and mindfulness*, Ebury Press, Australia, p. 65.

Chapter 8

1. Lowes & Tiggemann (2003) cited in Pai, S & Schryver, K 2015, *Children, Teens, Media, and Body Image*, Common Sense Media, p. 5, <https://www.commonsensemedia.org/research/children-teens-media-and-body-image>.
2. Hayes & Tantleff-Dunn (2010) cited in Pai & Schryver 2015, p. 5.
3. Baker, J 2014, *Change your world, not your body*, Tedx Talks, 14 July, YouTube, <https://www.youtube.com/watch?v=iSjwdN9vW0g>.
4. Butterfly Foundation 2019, 'Body image concerns need national response for young Australians', <https://butterfly.org.au/news/body-image-concerns-need-national-response-for-young-australians/>; Fildes, J, Robbins, A, Cave, L, Perrens, B & Wearring, A 2014, *Youth Survey 2014*, Mission Australia, p. 97.
5. Byrd-Bredbenner, Murray & Schlussel (2005), cited in Pai & Schryver 2015, p. 5.

Chapter 9

1. Telford, RM, Telford, RD, Olive, L, Cochrane, T, & Davey, R 2016, 'Why are girls less physically active than boys? Findings from the LOOK Longitudinal Study', *PLoS ONE*, vol. 11, no. 3, p. 1, <https://doi.org/10.1371/journal.pone.0150041>.

2. Shute, N 2013, 'Want your daughter to be science whiz? Soccer might help', NPR, <https://www.npr.org/sections/health-shots/2013/10/22/239692851/want-your-daughter-to-be-a-science-whiz-soccer-might-help/>.
3. Turnbull, D 2020, *50 Risks to Take With Your Kids,* Hardie Grant, Sydney, p. 16.
4. Whitebread, D, Neale, D, Jensen, H, Liu, C, Solis, SL, Hopkins, H, Hirsh-Pasek, K & Zosh, JM 2017, *The Role of Play in Children's Development: A review of the evidence,* The Lego Foundation, Billund, Denmark, p. 32, <https://www.legofoundation.com/media/1065/play-types-_-development-review_web.pdf>.
5. Grose, J 2020, 'The state of play: The act of playing shapes how our children see the world', *The New York Times*, 21 July, <https://www.nytimes.com/2020/07/21/parenting/the-state-of-play.html>.

Chapter 10

1. Australian Curriculum, Assessment and Reporting Authority (ACARA) 2013, NAPLAN Year 5 Language Conventions, p. 11, question 46, <https://acaraweb.blob.core.windows.net/acaraweb/docs/default-source/assessment-and-reporting-publications/naplan-2013-final-test-language-conventions-year-5.pdf?sfvrsn=2>.
2. ACARA 2016, NAPLAN Year 5 Numeracy, p. 5, question 11, <https://acaraweb.blob.core.windows.net/acaraweb/docs/default-source/assessment-and-reporting-publications/e5-naplan-2016-final-test-numeracy-year-5.pdf?sfvrsn=2>.

Chapter 11

1. Queensland Family and Child Commission (2018) cited in Vassallo, S, and Swami, N 2018, 'Tweens and teens: What do they worry about?', *Growing Up in Australia: The Longitudinal Study of Australian Children Annual Statistical Report 2018*, Australian Institute of Family Studies, pp. 133–4, <https://growingupinaustralia.gov.au/sites/default/files/publication-documents/lsac-asr-2018-chap12-worry.pdf>.
2. Brown, Teufel, Birch, & Kancheria (2006) cited in Vassallo & Swami 2018, p. 134.
3. Vassallo & Swami 2018, 'Tweens and teens', pp. 134, 137, 138.
4. Beyond Blue n.d., 'Anxiety management strategies', <https://www.beyondblue.org.au/the-facts/anxiety/treatments-for-anxiety/anxiety-management-strategies>.
5. University of Queensland 2020, 'One in five adolescents have suicidal thoughts or anxiety', *UQ News*, <https://www.uq.edu.au/news/article/2020/06/one-five-adolescents-have-suicidal-thoughts-or-anxiety>.

Chapter 12

1. This analogy was first provided by Jody Forbes, from Brisbane Girls Grammar School, while I was researching *Being 14*. King, M 2017, *Being 14*, Hachette Australia, Sydney, p. 201.
2. Influencer Marketing Hub 2020, 'Top Instagram influencers for 2020', <https://influencermarketinghub.com/top-instagram-influencers/>.
3. Influencer Marketing Hub 2020, *The State of Influencer Marketing 2020: Benchmark report*, <https://influencermarketinghub.com/influencer-marketing-benchmark-report-2020>.

Chapter 13

1. House of Representatives Standing Committee on Health, Aged Care and Sport 2019, *Bedtime Reading: An inquiry into sleep health awareness in Australia*, Parliament of the Commonwealth of Australia, pp. iii, 12, 13, 18, <https://parlinfo.aph.gov.au/parlInfo/download/committees/reportrep/024220/toc_pdf/BedtimeReading.pdf;fileType=application%2Fpdf>.

Chapter 14

1. Braun Research (2014) cited in Breheny Wallace, J 2015, 'Why children need chores', *The Wall Street Journal*, 13 March, <https://www.wsj.com/articles/why-children-need-chores-1426262655>.
2. Julian, K 2020, 'What happened to American childhood?', *The Atlantic Monthly*, <https://www.theatlantic.com/magazine/archive/2020/05/childhood-in-an-anxious-age/609079/>.
3. Paul Dillon in an interview, referring to studies such as Kuntsche, E & Kuntsche, S 2019, 'Parental drinking and characteristics of family life as predictors of preschoolers' alcohol-related knowledge and norms', *Addictive Behaviors*, vol. 88, pp. 92–8, <https://doi.org/10.1016/j.addbeh.2018.08.024> and Voogt, C, Beusink, M, Kleinjan, M, Otten, R, Engels, R, Smit, K & Kuntsche, E 2017, 'Alcohol-related cognitions in children (aged 2–10) and how they are shaped by parental alcohol use: A systematic review', *Drug and Alcohol Dependence*, vol. 177, pp. 277–90, <http://dx.doi.org/10.1016/j.drugalcdep.2017.04.006>.

Chapter 15

1. Australian Bureau of Statistics 2019, *Marriages and divorces, Australia* (reference period 2018), <https://www.abs.gov.au/statistics/people/people-and-communities/marriages-and-divorces-australia/latest-release#divorces>.

Chapter 16

1. Baxter, J 2018, 'Who do adolescents spend their time with?' *The Longitudinal Study of Australian Children Annual Statistical Report 2017*, Australian Institute of Family Studies, p. 26, <https:// growingupinaustralia.gov.au/sites/default/files/publication-documents/ lsac-asr-2017-chap4.pdf>.

Chapter 17

1. Marlay, B, Attenborough, J & Kutcher, V 2020, *Living in Limbo*, UNICEF Australia, Sydney, p. 2, <https://www.unicef.org.au/ Upload/UNICEF/Media/Documents/UNICEF-COVID-19-Living-in-Limbo-2020.pdf>.
2. McCrindle, M 2020, *The Future of Education*, Education Future Forum, p. 5, <https://mccrindle.com.au/wp-content/uploads/reports/ Education-Future-Report-2020.pdf>.
3. Wilson, R & Mude, W 2020, '"We had no sanitiser, no soap and minimal toilet paper": Here's how teachers feel about going back to the classroom', *The Conversation*, 14 May, <https://theconversation. com/we-had-no-sanitiser-no-soap-and-minimal-toilet-paper-heres-how-teachers-feel-about-going-back-to-the-classroom-138600>.
4. McCrindle 2020, *The Future of Education*, p. 13.

Chapter 18

1. Morgan, PJ, Young, MD, Barnes, AT, Eather, N, Pollock, ER & Lubans, DR 2019, 'Engaging fathers to increase physical activity in girls: The "dads and daughters exercising and empowered" (DADEE) randomized controlled trial', *Annals of Behavioral Medicine*, vol. 53, no. 1, <https://academic.oup.com/abm/ article-abstract/53/1/39/4965811>.
2. Baxter, J 2018, 'Who do adolescents spend their time with?', p. 33.
3. Yu, M & Baxter, J 2018, 'Relationships between parents and young teens', *The Longitudinal Study of Australian Children Annual Statistical Report 2017*, Institute of Family Studies, Melbourne, p. 36, <https://growingupinaustralia. gov.au/research-findings/annual-statistical-report-2017/ relationships-between-parents-and-young-teens>.

Acknowledgements

The idea for this book came from a group of mothers who had fourteen-year-old daughters. They'd read one of my previous books – *Being 14* – and wrote to ask more about the genesis of that particularly tricky age. Could it be that the eye-rolls started earlier than fourteen? How could they curb the anxiety that was robbing their precious daughter of tween sleep? Why couldn't their ten-year-old learn to make *real* friends? When did this awkward teen girl journey start? When? Could it possibly be at ten?

This book is the answer to those questions, and many more – and I owe it to the nine- and ten- and eleven-year-old girls who opened their hearts and told me what was going on inside their heads. In surveys and interviews, focus groups and school chats, online and in person, their brutal honesty shone. Thank you. I promised you I'd try to give you a voice in this book, and I hope I haven't disappointed. I've also kept the confidences I promised, so while all girls' names have been changed, every situation in this book remains real, as do the girls' comments. Just as real and raw is the advice of those experts who took the time to explain how we might guide our daughters through a calmer adolescent transition. Once again, I applaud the minds and the hearts of those who run our schools, and those who teach in them. It is a calling, but one that deserves so much more recognition that it currently boasts. Our girls are walking into school grounds each day, led by fierce, loyal leaders who want them to reach for the stars.

Thanks also to those researchers, scientists, psychologists, doctors, authors and other experts who answered my questions, over and over. I hope *Ten-ager* makes your job a touch easier too. The professionals who work in this area don't go searching for accolades, but they deserve so many. A special thanks to my friend Rebecca Sparrow, an author who spends her days helping our teens – and their parents – answer tricky questions, including through her podcast *Ask Me Anything*. Her advice has been invaluable. So has the advice of Angela White, from Adolescent Success, and Loren Bridge, from the Alliance of Girls' Schools Australasia. Our daughters benefit from the wealth of work, knowledge and research held by those organisations.

To the team at Hachette, especially Vanessa Radnidge, thank you. Vanessa's enthusiasm is infectious and she has the ability to make you want to meet deadline, with a smile on your face. To my editor Rebecca Allen, copyeditor Susan Gray and proofreader Susan Jarvis, *Ten-ager* is better because you've worked so hard at making it better. Every word is as important to you as it is to me. And to

Majella Dwan and her eagle eye for spelling mistakes, thank you. Christa Moffitt designed the book's cover, and it captures perfectly the girls who are at the heart of *Ten-ager*. Emily Lighezzolo, Eve Le Gall, Melissa Wilson and Emma Rusher have the job of publicity and marketing in a world where a pandemic has turned those things on their head, but are driven by ideas, not tradition, and it's awesome to watch, and learn. And to the rest of the team at Hachette, because a book really is a team game, thank you – especially Jenny Topham, Fiona Hazard, Isabel Staas, Daniel Pilkington, and Louise Sherwin-Stark. I keep walking back through Hachette's doors because you make the task of a reporter and writer so enjoyable.

Finally, this book was written during a fairly turbulent time in my family, with COVID19 providing some challenges and my husband's heart attack providing others. Like so many other families, 2020 was a lesson in what's important. To David, the love of my life, thank you for being both my front stop and back stop. And finally, to our two precious teen girls, Maddie and Siena. You make everything I do better. What would you think, now I've finally finished this, if I turned my attention to studying sixteen and seventeen-year-old girls?

Index